THE
INDUSTRIAL
REVOLUTION

WITH **25** PROJECTS

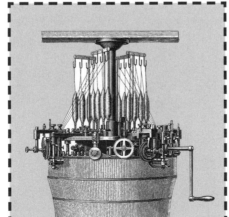

INVESTIGATE HOW SCIENCE AND TECHNOLOGY CHANGED THE WORLD

CARLA MOONEY

Illustrated by Jen Vaughn

Titles in the **Build It Yourself** Series

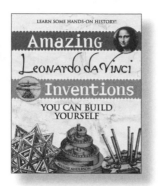

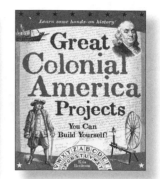

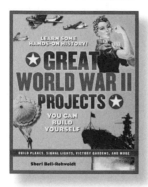

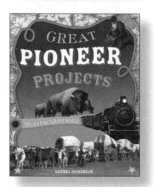

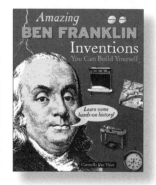

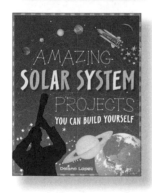

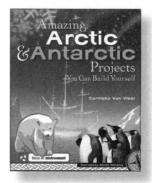

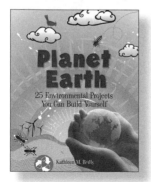

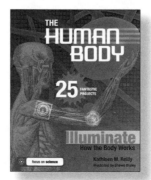

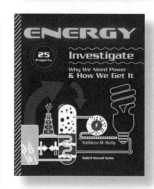

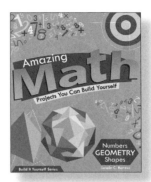

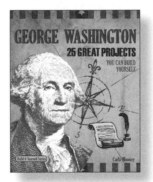

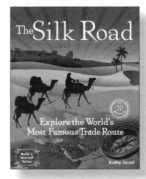

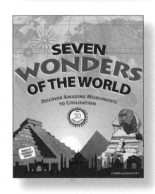

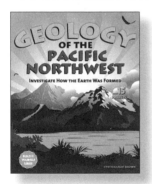

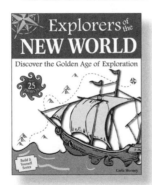

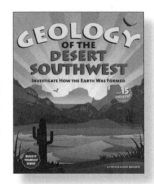

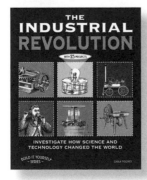

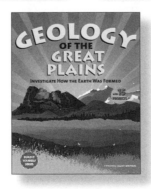

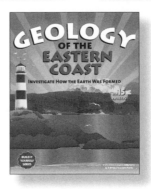

Nomad Press is committed to preserving ancient forests and natural resources. We elected to print *The Industrial Revolution: Investigate How Science and Technology Changed the World* on 4,007 lbs. of Williamsburg Recycled 30% offset.

Nomad Press made this paper choice because our printer, Sheridan Books, is a member of Green Press Initiative, a nonprofit program dedicated to supporting authors, publishers, and suppliers in their efforts to reduce their use of fiber obtained from endangered forests.

For more information, visit **www.greenpressinitiative.org**

This book was manufactured by Sheridan Books,
Ann Arbor, MI USA.
July 2011, Job #328492
ISBN: 978-1-936313-81-5

Illustrations by Jen Vaughn
Educational Consultant, Marla Conn

Questions regarding the ordering of this book should be addressed to
Independent Publishers Group
814 N. Franklin St.
Chicago, IL 60610
www.ipgbook.com

Nomad Press
2456 Christian St.
White River Junction, VT 05001
www.nomadpress.net

CONTENTS

Spinning Jenny

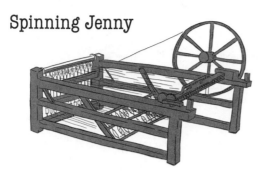

1712: Thomas Newcomen invents the first steam engine.

1733: John Kay invents the flying shuttle.

1765: James Watt builds the first practical steam engine.

1767: James Hargreaves invents the spinning jenny.

1769: Richard Arkwright invents the spinning frame.

1790: John Fitch operates a passenger steamboat service on the Delaware River.

1790: Samuel Slater opens the first American cotton mill in Pawtucket, Rhode Island.

1790: The United States passes its first patent law and grants the first patent to Samuel Hopkins.

1793: Eli Whitney invents the cotton gin, a machine that removes seeds from cotton.

1807: Robert Fulton launches the *Clermont*, the first commercially successful steamboat.

1813: Francis Cabot Lowell forms the Boston Manufacturing Company.

1825: The Erie Canal opens.

1841: The National Road reaches Vandalia, Illinois.

1844: Samuel Morse sends the first telegraph message using Morse code.

1856: Henry Bessemer designs a process to turn iron ore into steel.

1860: Shoemakers strike in Lynn, Massachusetts.

1866: The National Labor Union is formed.

Oil Gusher

Steamboat

1869: The Central Pacific and Union Pacific railroads meet at Promontory Summit, Utah.

1870: John D. Rockefeller forms the Standard Oil Company.

1875: Andrew Carnegie opens his first steel mill in Pittsburgh, Pennsylvania.

1876: The Centennial Exhibition in Philadelphia, Pennsylvania, displays America's inventions.

1876: Alexander Graham Bell invents the telephone.

1877: A violent strike erupts after railroad wages are cut.

1877: Thomas Edison develops the phonograph for playing recorded music.

1879: Thomas Edison invents the incandescent light bulb.

1882: Thomas Edison opens the first electric power station in New York.

1885: The first skyscraper is built in Chicago.

1885: German engineer Gottlieb Daimler improves the internal combustion engine and builds vehicles powered by it.

1886: The American Federation of Labor is established.

1890: Congress passes the Sherman Antitrust Act and outlaws monopolies.

1892: A violent strike breaks out at the Homestead Steelworks in Pittsburgh.

1908: Henry Ford begins producing the Model T.

1913: The Ford Motor Company uses a moving assembly line to produce cars.

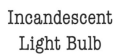

Incandescent Light Bulb

INTRODUCTION

Ideas, Invention, and Innovation

If you could go back in time a couple of hundred years or so, you'd find that the world was a very different place than it is today. Most people lived a farmer's life. They grew their own food and made almost everything by hand.

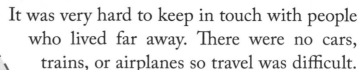

WORDS TO KNOW

innovation: a new invention or way of doing something.

Industrial Revolution: a time of far-reaching change when the large-scale production of goods began.

manufacture: to make something by machine, in a large factory.

goods: things for sale or to use.

factory: a place where goods are made.

It was very hard to keep in touch with people who lived far away. There were no cars, trains, or airplanes so travel was difficult. There were no telephones or telegraphs, so news had to be carried from town to town by travelers or messengers. People relied on themselves and their small communities.

But then things started to change. From the late 1700s through the early 1900s, many new ideas, inventions, and **innovations** dramatically affected the way people lived and worked. We call this period of great change the **Industrial Revolution**.

DURING THE INDUSTRIAL REVOLUTION, MACHINES STARTED DOING THE WORK OF PEOPLE. THESE MACHINES COULD **MANUFACTURE GOODS** FASTER AND MORE CHEAPLY THAN EVER.

Great **factories** full of machines sprung up in towns and cities, attracting workers from the farms. Steam engines and railroads carried goods to people who lived far away. Meanwhile, inventions such as electricity and the telephone transformed daily life, bringing people closer together. The Industrial Revolution began in Britain, but it soon spread to Europe and the United States.

WORDS TO KNOW

profit: to make money from business or investments.

rural: in the country.

urban: in the city.

working class: people who work in factories and in jobs using their hands.

slum: a run-down place to live.

labor union: a group of workers that bargains with the people they work for.

bargain: to work to reach an agreement.

wage: payment for work.

INDUSTRY IS THE PRODUCTION OF GOODS, ESPECIALLY IN FACTORIES.

In many ways, the Industrial Revolution improved life for people around the world. It became easier to produce goods, communicate, and travel. Those who **profited** from the inventions and innovations of this age enjoyed wealth.

But for others, especially those who worked in the factories, life was not as easy. Many found the transition from a **rural** to an **urban** lifestyle difficult. The **working class** often struggled, living in filthy **slums** and working at dangerous jobs. **Labor unions** emerged to protect workers. These unions **bargained** with factory owners for better working conditions and better **wages**.

This book will help you discover the legendary time of the Industrial Revolution. You'll learn about the inventors and their inventions, a little history of the time in which they lived, some interesting facts about the people and places around them, and how the Industrial Revolution changed everyday life.

Most of the projects in this book can be made with little adult supervision, using materials you already have at home or can easily find at a craft store. So get ready to step back in time and discover the Industrial Revolution!

CHAPTER ONE

A Revolution Begins with Textiles

In the early 1700s, **textiles** were made in people's homes. Cloth **merchants** brought wool, cotton, or **flax** fibers to spinners who worked at home. The spinners used a spinning wheel to spin the fibers into thread. Next, the merchants took the thread to a weaver, who used a loom to weave it into cloth. This cloth could then be sold at a market. Each step in the process was slow and required a lot of human labor. The entire process had changed little over the centuries.

At this time, there was a population explosion in England and Europe. More people meant a greater **demand** for cheap clothing. But home-based weavers and spinners worked too slowly to keep up with the increased demand. Cloth merchants realized that they could make a lot of money if they could speed up the cloth-making process.

THE TRANSFORMATION OF THE
TEXTILE INDUSTRY BEGAN
THE INDUSTRIAL REVOLUTION.

WORDS TO KNOW

textile: cloth or fabric.

merchant: someone who buys and sells goods.

flax: a plant with blue flowers whose fibers are used to make linen.

demand: the amount that people want to buy.

mining: taking minerals from the ground, such as iron ore.

natural resource: materials that occur in nature, such as oil, coal, water, and land.

WHY BRITAIN?

Why was the Industrial Revolution born in Great Britain? British inventors were the first to improve the textile and **mining** industries. They dug canals, built railroads, and created the world's first real factories.

Many historians believe that conditions in eighteenth-century Britain were perfect to launch the new machines, processes, and way of life of the Industrial Revolution. Britain had a large supply of **natural resources** like coal and iron that could be used in manufacturing. Britain also had many rivers that could move newly manufactured goods. In addition, Britain had a large labor force that could be put to work in factories. Finally, the British empire already had a strong system of banking, credit, and insurance. These tools made it easy for manufacturers to borrow and lend money easily and to do business with each other. ⊕

With this **incentive**, several **enterprising** Englishmen worked to build machines that could make cloth better and faster. The result was a series of inventions that transformed the entire cloth-making process, and made textiles the first industry to step into the Industrial Revolution.

▪ John Kay and the Flying Shuttle ▪

The flying shuttle was the first machine to **revolutionize** the textile industry. A shuttle was a needlelike device that weavers used to push thread from one side of a loom to the other. This was done by hand. If the looms were large, two weavers pushed the shuttle back and forth to each other.

In 1733, an Englishman named John Kay improved the weaving process by inventing a flying shuttle. Instead of pushing the shuttle by hand, a single weaver could simply pull a cord or lever to throw the shuttle across the loom. This allowed the weaver to produce almost twice as much cloth. A single weaver could work a large loom alone.

But the flying shuttle worked too well. Weavers used thread faster than spinners could spin it. So weavers were often forced to sit **idle**, waiting for more thread. Now cloth merchants had to find a way to speed up the spinning process.

WORDS TO KNOW

incentive: the possibility of a reward that encourages people to do something or work harder.

enterprising: willing to try a new, risky project.

revolutionize: to bring about a far-reaching change.

idle: not working.

- - James Hargreaves and the Spinning Jenny - -

James Hargreaves was an English weaver from Blackburn who was frustrated by the thread shortages. Historians believe he stumbled on the idea for a faster spinning machine when his wife accidentally tipped over her spinning wheel. The **spindle** landed in an upright position and continued to spin.

When Hargreaves saw the horizontal spinning wheel on the ground, an idea hatched in his mind. What if several spindles were placed upright and side-by-side? If such a machine could be built, Hargreaves reasoned that it might be possible for a single spinner to work several spindles at the same time. This would dramatically increase the amount of thread a spinner could produce.

WORDS TO KNOW

spindle: the rod on a spinning wheel that twists the thread. The twisted thread is wound around the rod.

DID YOU KNOW?

Unmarried daughters usually spun yarn or thread in the family home. So the name "spinster" was commonly used to describe an unmarried woman.

FOR SEVERAL YEARS, HARGREAVES WORKED TO TRANSFER HIS IDEA INTO A WORKING MACHINE, WHICH HE NAMED THE SPINNING JENNY.

The jenny had six spindles placed on their sides. They were all attached to each other and turned by one large wheel. Instead of just one thread, this simple wooden machine spun several threads at once. Now one spinner could do the work of many!

At first, Hargreaves kept his spinning jenny secret. However, once he sold a few models for money, word quickly spread about his fantastic new machine. Merchants and weavers were excited by the large amounts of thread the spinning jenny could produce.

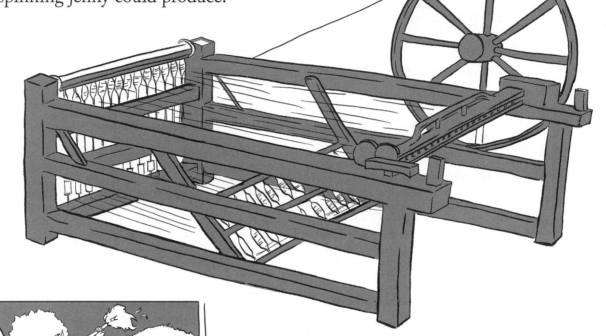

NOT EVERYONE WAS PLEASED WITH HARGREAVES'S JENNY.

Local spinners feared that the machine would take work away from them. An angry mob stormed Hargreaves's house, destroyed his workshop, and smashed all the spinning jennies they found. Afraid for his family's safety, Hargreaves left Blackburn and moved to the town of Nottingham.

In Nottingham, Hargreaves set up a new shop and obtained a **patent** in 1770 for the spinning jenny. Unfortunately, his patent was too late. Manufacturers were already copying the spinning jenny and refused to pay any **royalty** to Hargreaves. Soon, textile manufacturers were building spinning jennies with 20 spindles, and then 100 spindles!

IN THE END, HARGREAVES RECEIVED NEXT TO NOTHING FOR HIS INVENTION THAT COMPLETELY REVOLUTIONIZED ENGLAND'S TEXTILE INDUSTRY.

WORDS TO KNOW

patent: a right given to only one inventor to manufacture, use, or sell an invention for a certain number of years.

royalty: money paid to the inventor of something to use or sell the invention.

Richard Arkwright and the Water Frame

With all these inventions, the entire cloth-making process was much faster and cheaper. But weavers and spinners still complained about a shortage of thread. A traveling wigmaker, Richard Arkwright, saw the opportunity to make money in textiles. With the help of clockmaker John Kay, Arkwright set out to improve the mechanical spinning machine so that it could make stronger yarn with less labor.

DID YOU KNOW?

Before John Kay's flying shuttle, a single home weaver could use the thread spun by two or three spinners. With a flying shuttle, the same weaver used the thread spun by eight or more spinners.

Several years of work resulted in the invention of a large spinning machine that used a water wheel to turn wooden rollers at different speeds and twist **carded cotton** onto multiple spindles. The result was a stronger cotton thread that was perfect for **warp**.

IN 1769, ARKWRIGHT RECEIVED HIS FIRST PATENT FOR THE WATER FRAME.

WORDS TO KNOW

carded cotton: cotton that is cleaned and brushed to prepare it for spinning.

warp: the strong thread that runs vertically in a loom.

At the mill, Arkwright set up a brand-new system of divided labor, giving each worker a specific task. The tasks did not require much skill and kids as young as 10 worked at his mill. They worked from six in the morning until seven at night, with half an hour off for breakfast and 40 minutes for dinner. They got their education in church on Sundays.

DID YOU KNOW?

Many court cases challenged Arkwright's patents as copies of other inventors. There is still debate as to whether he truly invented the water frame, or simply found a good way to use it.

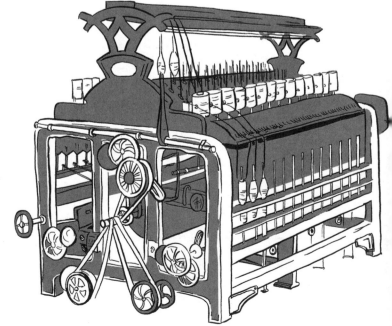

THE NAME . . . WATER FRAME

After attempting to use horsepower to spin his machines, Arkwright built a factory on the riverbanks near Derbyshire. The force of the river's current turned a large paddle wheel that was connected to the spinning machines' crank. This waterpower gave Arkwright's spinning machine its name—the spinning water frame. ⊕

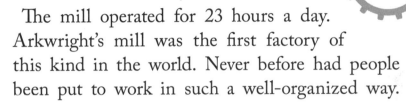

The mill operated for 23 hours a day. Arkwright's mill was the first factory of this kind in the world. Never before had people been put to work in such a well-organized way. Never had people been told to come in at a certain time in the morning, and work all day at a specific task.

ARKWRIGHT BECAME KNOWN AS THE FATHER OF THE FACTORY SYSTEM.

As the demand for cotton thread grew, Arkwright built additional mills. Meanwhile, local spinners feared the changes that Arkwright and his mills brought. Angry mobs attacked his mills, burning a mill in Chorley to the ground. Yet Arkwright argued that his mills were important because they gave jobs to the working poor.

DID YOU KNOW?

When local spinners and weavers refused to work in Arkwright's factories, he hired poor children and orphans. By 1790, Arkwright's mills employed as many as 5,000 people.

Even though many people were afraid of the change, Richard Arkwright's factories transformed the textile industry. More than any other man, he combined power, machinery, and labor to create the modern factory system.

Seeing Arkwright's success, many wealthy businessmen invested in textiles, looking to make a large profit. Soon textile factories dotted the banks of rivers and streams throughout England. At first, the rivers powered the mill machinery. Eventually, factories would turn to another invention for power, the steam engine.

WORDS TO KNOW

automated: to operate by machine instead of human labor.

— — Edmund Cartwright and the Power Loom — —

In 1784, Edmund Cartwright visited one of Richard Arkwright's factories and watched machines spin thread faster and stronger than ever before. He realized that an **automated** weaving machine could further improve the cloth-making process. By 1785, Cartwright had a patent for his first version of a water-powered loom. His power loom could weave thread into cloth much faster than a home weaver could weave. It was also much larger than the typical home loom so Cartwright needed a factory to hold his looms. After making a few improvements to the power loom, Cartwright opened a weaving mill in Doncaster in 1787.

SAMUEL CROMPTON AND THE SPINNING MULE

Even with these improvements in the cloth-making process, there was still one more problem preventing the manufacture of cheap clothes. Weavers had to use two different types of threads—cotton and linen. Cotton thread was cheaper, but it was weak, so linen thread had to be added for strength. To make clothes cheaper, someone had to find a way to make cotton thread stronger.

In 1779, Samuel Crompton invented a spinning machine he called the mule. The mule combined the moving carriage of the spinning jenny with the roller of the water frame. It spun strong, fine, soft yarn that could be used for all types of textiles.

Neighbors became curious as to what Crompton was doing to create such high-quality thread. Visitors stopped by his house at all hours, hoping to catch a glimpse of his machine. When some people tried to spy in his windows, Crompton put up screens to block their view.

Finally, the stress of trying to keep his secret became too much, so Crompton sold the rights to his invention to a manufacturer. Soon textile manufacturers were building larger versions of Crompton's mule that had as many as 400 spindles. Crompton made no money from these sales. ⊕

The Steam Engine

Using water to power machinery was a great step forward, but there was a problem. Factory owners could only build their factories near rivers and streams. To make it possible to build factories anywhere in England, a different power source was necessary. It had to be both inexpensive and reliable.

Some inventors believed that steam power was the answer. Thomas Newcomen had invented the first **commercially** successful steam engine in 1712. His engine burned coal, which heated water until it produced steam that was powerful enough to turn a machine's gears and **turbines**. Newcomen's steam engine was mainly used to pump water from coal mines, which allowed miners to dig deeper into the earth.

In 1765, a Scottish inventor and instrument maker named James Watt was asked to repair a Newcomen steam engine. While doing so, he realized that the engine was extremely **inefficient**. It lost too much steam as it worked.

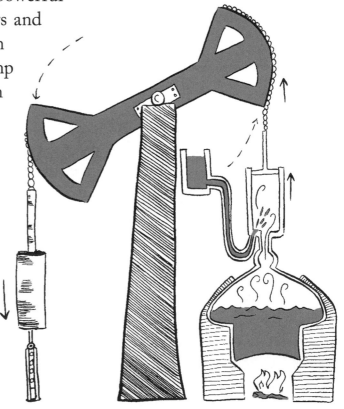

WORDS TO KNOW

commercially: profitable, to be sold.

turbine: a machine with blades turned by the force of water, air, or steam.

inefficient: wasting time or energy.

Watt decided to make several changes to the steam engine. The result was an engine that produced more power from the same amount of coal. Together with his business partner, John Roebuck, Watt manufactured and sold steam engines. Soon all of England was steaming into the Industrial Age.

Changing Way of Life

With factories spreading across England, life began to change. Factories needed workers, and many people left their rural communities to work in towns and cities. Although these people were used to working long hours at home, working in a factory was much different. At home, workers could schedule their own hours and take breaks when they wanted to. In a factory, supervisors kept workers on a tight schedule. Few breaks were allowed. Bosses told workers when it was time to eat or drink.

WORDS TO KNOW

entrepreneur: a person who starts a business.

mass produce: to manufacture large amounts of a product.

DID YOU KNOW?

A single steam engine could help produce as much thread in 12 hours as 750 human spinners could spin in a year!

MANY WORKERS FOUND FACTORY WORK TIRING AND BORING, BUT THEY NEEDED THE JOB TO SUPPORT THEIR FAMILIES.

Entrepreneurs from other industries saw how the textile business was booming because of factories. So they built their own factories. By 1800, England was home to factories **mass producing** items such as pottery, spoons, buttons, buckles, and teapots. It would not take long for the Industrial Revolution to spread to the rest of Europe and the United States.

MAKE YOUR OWN
Knitting Spool

Before the power loom was invented, weaving and knitting were slow, tedious tasks. Try hand weaving with your own knitting spool. With a few simple items and some yarn, you can create a knitted tube that you could use as a bracelet, belt, or skinny scarf!

1 Tape one craft stick against the outside of a cardboard tube, letting it stick out 1 to 2 inches from the edge.

2 Tape a second craft stick directly across from the first stick. Tape the other four sticks evenly around the tube.

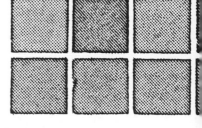

3 To begin knitting, take the end of your yarn and tape it to the inside of the tube to anchor it. Wrap the yarn clockwise around one stick.

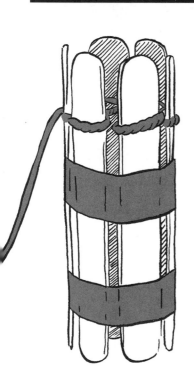

4 Turn the tube clockwise by one stick and wrap the yarn clockwise around the next stick. Keep turning and wrapping until each stick has one loop wrapped around it. This is your foundation.

5 Begin the second row by wrapping your next loop above the first loop, closer to the end of the stick. Use a pencil, crochet hook, or your fingers to lift the first loop over the second loop. Lift it over the end of the popsicle stick, dropping it into the center of the tube.

6 Keep going, wrapping each stick clockwise and turning the tube clockwise. Each time, pull the lower stitch over the new stitch and off the stick. Your knitted piece will slowly work its way toward the bottom of your tube.

7 Continue knitting until you reach the length you want. To cast off, lift one stitch off its stick and slide it onto the stick next to it. Lift the bottom stitch over the top stitch. Moving clockwise, move the stitch to the next stick. Keep repeating until there is one stitch left.

8 Cut the yarn, leaving a few inches. Thread the yarn tail through the last loop and pull tightly. Weave the yarn tails into the finished piece.

WORDS TO KNOW

irrigation: supplying water to farmland.

aristocrat: a member of a ruling or wealthy class of people.

AGRICULTURAL REVOLUTION

If people didn't like working in factories, why couldn't they work on farms instead? Because before the Industrial Revolution there was a revolution in British agriculture. Vast improvements in planting, crop rotation, and **irrigation** helped farmers grow more food and feed more people. But it also meant that fewer workers were needed on farms. As farming became more profitable, British **aristocrats** bought more and more land. By 1815, large landowners had fenced off more than a million acres. Without land to work, small farmers became the source of labor for factories and industry. ⊕

WEAVE WITH YOUR OWN
Hand Loom

People used to make cloth by hand using hand looms. They worked at home and used their cloth for their family's clothing, bedding, and other items. Some sold their cloth to merchants.

SUPPLIES
• • • • • • • • • • • • •

⊗ cardboard, about 8 by 10 inches (20 by 25 centimeters)

⊗ scissors

⊗ yarn, several colors

⊗ tape

⊗ long yarn needle

⊗ wide-toothed comb

1 To make your loom, take the cardboard and cut notches close together along the two short sides. The notches should be ¼ inch long (½ centimeter) and no more than ¼ inch apart (½ centimeter).

2 Cut a piece of yarn approximately 3 feet long (1 meter). Tape one end of the yarn to the back of the loom and pull it through one of the end slits in your cardboard loom.

3 Loop the yarn tightly down to the first notch on the bottom of the card. Wind it around the back of the card and back up to the second notch at the top. Continue winding your yarn through all the notches on your card. Keep your yarn tight. When you wind through the last notch, tape the yarn to anchor this end to the loom. These strings will be the warp threads on your loom.

4 Now that your loom is ready, it's time to weave! Cut about 2 feet (½ meter) from one color of yarn and thread it into your needle. Weave your needle under the first string on your loom, then over the next.

DID YOU KNOW?

In 1799, a factory that had just purchased 400 of Edmund Cartwright's power looms burned to the ground. It is suspected that the fire was set by workers who feared they would lose their jobs to the machines.

Continue across the loom in this under and over pattern. Once you've reached the end, turn your needle back in the opposite direction, and weave back across the loom. If you wove under the last string, weave the yarn over it this time as you weave back to the other side of the loom.

5 Continue weaving across the loom. Make sure you don't pull the thread too tightly or your cloth strip will curl inwards. As you finish a row, use your comb to push the new row against the completed rows.

6 To change colors or add more yarn, tie a knot joining the two strands of yarn. Make sure your knot is at the end of a row, not in the middle. Push the knot through to the back of the weaving so it doesn't show. Trim any excess pieces close to the knot. Continue weaving and alternating colors until you reach the length you want. When you finish weaving, tie the end of your last piece of yarn to an end loom string.

7 Cut the loom strings on the back of your loom in the middle. Knot pairs of loom strings close to the weaving to prevent your weaving from slipping apart. Trim the loose strings close to the knots.

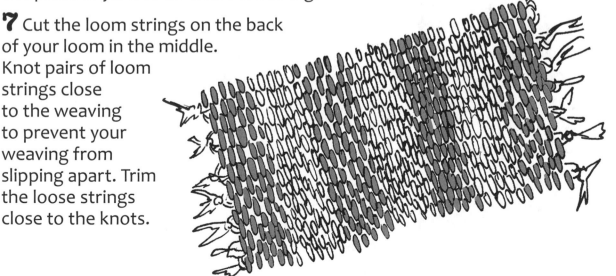

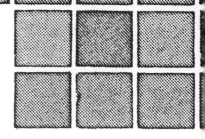

MAKE YOUR OWN
Oatmeal–Honey Soap

SUPPLIES
. . . .

- ✹ bar of plain white soap and its box
- ✹ cheese grater
- ✹ wax paper
- ✹ measuring cups
- ✹ heat resistant glass bowl
- ✹ water
- ✹ spoon
- ✹ stove
- ✹ pot
- ✹ empty soap box
- ✹ scissors
- ✹ petroleum jelly
- ✹ ¼ cup uncooked oatmeal (60 milliliters)
- ✹ 1 tablespoon honey
- ✹ 1 teaspoon almond oil

Before the Industrial Revolution, people made everything they needed at home, including soap. Instead of buying a bar of specialty soap, transform a simple white bar of soap at home with this easy recipe!

1 Grate the white soap over a piece of wax paper until you have ¾ cup grated (180 milliliters). Put the grated soap in the glass bowl. Add ¼ cup water (60 milliliters) and stir gently.

2 With an adult's supervision, simmer a pot of water on the stove over low heat. Place the glass bowl over the pot of simmering water and heat gently until the soap melts, about 10 minutes. Do not stir, or you will add bubbles to your soap.

3 While your soap is melting, cut the top off the empty soap box. This will be your soap mold. Spread a thin layer of petroleum jelly on the inside of the box so that your soap will not stick to the sides.

4 When your soap is melted, remove the glass bowl from the heat. Add oatmeal, honey, and almond oil. Stir gently to mix. Pour your soap into the soap-box mold. Put it in the refrigerator to set.

5 Once the soap has set, remove it from the refrigerator and peel off the box. Place the soap on a cookie rack for about three weeks to completely dry. Then cut or package it to give away as a gift.

MAKE YOUR OWN
Water-Powered Wheel

Early textile factories were often built near rivers. Water-powered wheels turned gears and ran factory machinery. You can build a simple version to see how running water turns a wheel.

SUPPLIES

- 1 pencil
- 2 plastic plates
- masking tape
- 6 plastic cups, 8- or 9-ounce size
- 1 wooden dowel, at least 12 inches long (30 centimeters)

1 Using a pencil, punch a hole in the center of each plastic plate.

2 Attach the plates bottom to bottom, using rolled-up masking tape and also taping them together around the inside edge. Make sure your center holes are lined up.

3 Tape the plastic cups around the edge of the plates. Make sure all the cups are placed the long way and in the same direction.

4 Slide the wooden dowel through the holes in the center of the plates.

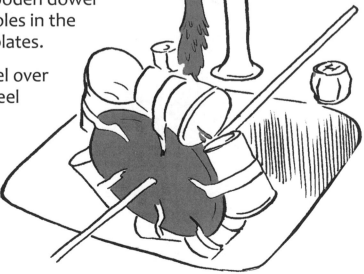

5 Hold the dowel and water wheel over a sink. Run the water over the wheel and watch it turn!

6 Try the project again, changing the size and number of cups on your wheel. Change the strength of the water stream. Do the changes affect how fast the water wheel turns?

CHAPTER TWO

The Industrial Revolution Comes to America

British manufactured goods were sold throughout Europe and in America. Because they were machine-made, these goods were cheaper than hand-made products. They sold very well. Noticing this, European and American businessmen decided to build their own profitable factories. Many of them travelled to Britain to discover how British **industrialists** did things.

WORDS TO KNOW

industrialist: someone who works with businesses and factories.

export: to send something to another country to be sold.

But Britain did not want to share its industrial innovations. Many companies tried to guard against spies. They built factories with thick walls and small windows to keep out unwelcome visitors. Some companies forced workers to swear that they would never tell anyone about their factory's manufacturing secrets.

The British government passed laws that made it illegal to **export** spinning or weaving machinery. They even made it illegal for machine operators to leave the country! For a short time, the British efforts to protect their secrets worked. Yet they could not stop the flow of knowledge forever. Eventually, the Industrial Revolution spread through Europe and to the United States.

PATENT LAWS

In the years leading up to the Industrial Revolution, there was no way for an inventor to protect his ideas and inventions from being stolen by another person. To protect inventors, the United States passed its first patent law in 1790. The law gave an inventor control over his idea or invention for 17 years. With this protection, people had more incentive to spend time creating new inventions. If successful, they could make money selling their inventions to businesses. If someone stole their idea without paying a royalty, the inventor could sue him in court for money lost. ⊕

- - Father of the American Industrial Revolution - -

The first person to bring knowledge of textile manufacturing to the United States was an Englishman named Samuel Slater. When he was 14, Slater became an **apprentice** and learned the textile manufacturing process. Soon he had learned enough to become a mill supervisor.

Meanwhile, the newly independent United States was determined to stop buying manufactured goods from Britain. American businessmen were willing to pay a lot of money to anyone who could help them set up a working textile factory. Slater realized that his knowledge of textile technology was valuable. He decided to help the Americans.

But leaving Britain would be tricky. Because Slater knew how to operate textile machines, it was against British law for him to leave the country. He could be thrown in jail if he was found leaving with drawings of textile machinery. Instead of drawing pictures of the machines, Slater memorized them. In 1789, Slater disguised himself as a farmer and boarded a ship headed for New York City.

When he arrived in the United States, Slater met Moses Brown, a merchant from Rhode Island. Using Brown's money and his own memory of English machinery, Slater built America's first water-powered, cotton-spinning mill in Pawtucket, Rhode Island.

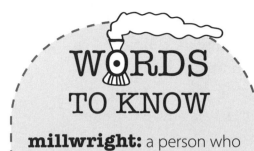

WORDS TO KNOW

millwright: a person who builds the machinery of a mill.

DID YOU KNOW?

Samuel Slater introduced the Rhode Island Method of hiring employees. Instead of individual workers, Slater would hire entire families, including children, to work in his mills. Workers lived in company-owned housing, shopped at company-owned stores, and studied in company-run schools.

By 1800, Slater's mill employed more than 100 workers. He built several more successful cotton mills throughout New England. Slater's mills became an important first step in the American Industrial Revolution. A generation of **millwrights** and textile workers trained in Slater's mills. By 1810, dozens of water-powered spinning mills could be found along the riverbanks of southern New England.

— Francis Cabot Lowell —

Although the New England mills spun thread, most weavers still worked at home. Typically, weavers picked up their yarn at the mills, wove it at home, and returned the finished cloth to the mill. This system was inefficient and slow.

On a trip to England in 1810, a Boston businessman named Francis Cabot Lowell toured British textile mills. He was impressed with their operation and how fast they wove cloth. While at the mill, Lowell memorized how English power looms worked. When he returned to the United States, Lowell hired a mechanic to build an improved version of the British loom.

NOW AMERICAN WEAVING COULD KEEP PACE WITH AMERICAN SPINNING.

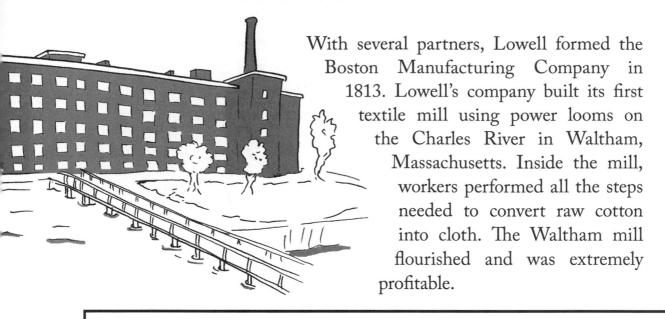

With several partners, Lowell formed the Boston Manufacturing Company in 1813. Lowell's company built its first textile mill using power looms on the Charles River in Waltham, Massachusetts. Inside the mill, workers performed all the steps needed to convert raw cotton into cloth. The Waltham mill flourished and was extremely profitable.

THE GREAT DEBATE

Not everyone in America was in favor of the Industrial Revolution. Two well-known politicians, Thomas Jefferson and Alexander Hamilton, were on different sides of the issue. As the Secretary of the Treasury, Hamilton believed that industrialization was important to help the new country's economy grow and compete with Europe. He knew that state-of-the-art factories would help the United States produce more goods.

Thomas Jefferson, who was George Washington's Secretary of State, disagreed. Jefferson wanted the United States to remain a rural, farming society. While visiting England, he had seen the poverty of workers and the dangerous factory conditions. He believed it was better for the United States to supply raw materials to English factories instead.

Although the debate between the two sides lasted for years, Hamilton's argument eventually won, and the United States government encouraged the Industrial Revolution to spread throughout the young nation. ⊕

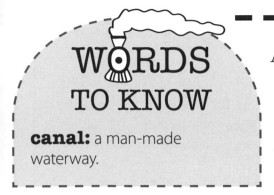

WORDS TO KNOW

canal: a man-made waterway.

━ ━ ━ ━ The Lowell Mills ━ ━ ━ ━

Although Lowell died in 1817, the Boston Company continued his work and expanded its textile manufacturing. In 1822, the company began constructing a huge new mill complex in a farming village on the Merrimack River, about 30 miles from Boston. They designed buildings and laid out streets. They built mills, machine shops, and housing for workers. They also built a series of **canals** to manage the river's waterpower. In honor of Lowell, the company named the town after him.

LOWELL BECAME THE COUNTRY'S FIRST PLANNED INDUSTRIAL TOWN, AND SOON IT WAS THE LARGEST INDUSTRIAL CENTER IN AMERICA.

MERRIMACK RIVER

PAWTUCKET FALLS

LOWELL, MA
about 1842
✪ = MILLS
▮ = CANALS

It employed more than 10,000 people and produced almost one million yards of cloth each week (914,400 meters). The sheer size of the city stunned visitors. Massive brick mills lined the Merrimack River for nearly a mile (1½ kilometers). The city's canals drove the waterwheels for 40 mill buildings. These waterwheels powered 320,000 spindles and almost 10,000 looms. Some visitors described the city as one of the wonders of the world.

DID YOU KNOW?

Lowell was called the spindle city because of its large textile industries.

MILL GIRLS OF LOWELL

Some of the first workers in the Lowell textile mills were young women. They were between 15 and 25 years old, and left their farms for better opportunities in the city. At the time, women had no property rights. A widow could be left without her husband's property. A daughter could be left with nothing when her father died. When this happened, a woman was either forced to marry or become a burden to her family. The textile factories opened up a new world of opportunities for these women. They could earn their own money and spend it how they wanted, without answering to anyone.

Mill work was long and hard. The girls worked up to 13-hour days in the factories and were

expected to follow strict schedules and codes of behavior. If a young woman did not have a relative to stay with, the mill required her to live in a boarding house. A typical boarding house held 30 to 40 women. Four to eight women shared each bedroom, and two women slept in each bed. **Chaperones** kept a watchful eye on the young women and reported any rule breaking.

The women formed a close-knit community. They wrote letters, sewed, played piano, and read and discussed newspapers, magazines, the Bible, and other literature. When the girls returned to their rural homes, they were often looked to for new fashions, books, and ideas from the big city. ⊕

WORDS TO KNOW

chaperone: an adult who protects the safety of young people and makes sure they behave well.

Eli Whitney and the Cotton Gin

As a young boy, Eli Whitney could often be found fiddling around in his father's workshop instead of finishing his farm chores. By age 12, he had made his own violin.

While visiting the South as a young man, Whitney listened to farmers complain that there was no profit in growing cotton. To prepare cotton, workers had to pick tiny green seeds from the cotton **boll** by hand. This was a long and tedious job, so southern planters grew very little cotton. But as cotton demand grew in northern textile factories and overseas, southern planters were itching to find a way to make cotton profitable.

> **THE IDEA OF MAKING A MACHINE TO REMOVE THE SEEDS FROM THE COTTON BOLL INTRIGUED WHITNEY.**

If Whitney could invent a machine to pick cotton seeds, he could apply for a patent and make a lot of money. He set to work and soon developed a cotton **gin** in 1793. His gin mechanically combed out the cotton's green seeds. A small gin could be cranked by hand, while larger gins could be powered by horses or water.

Whitney demonstrated his model to a few local planters. In one hour, Whitney processed as much cotton as it took several workers a full day to process. The planters realized Whitney's machine could turn cotton into a moneymaker. They immediately planted entire fields with cotton.

WORDS TO KNOW

boll: the seed pod of the cotton plant that fluffy cotton fibers burst out of.

gin: a tool or mechanical device.

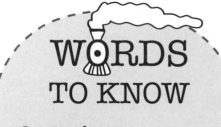

plantation: a large farm where crops are grown for sale.

The cotton gin ushered in the era of King Cotton in the American South. Cotton's enormous profits drove the growth of wealthy **plantations**. It also resulted in a huge increase in the number of southern slaves, who were needed more than ever to work the cotton fields. By 1850, the number of slaves had risen from 700,000 before the cotton gin to 3.2 million after it was invented.

INTERCHANGEABLE PARTS

During the Industrial Revolution, machines took over manufacturing. But without interchangeable parts, this transformation would not have been possible. Interchangeable parts are identical and can be substituted for each other. This meant that if something in a machine broke, a new part could replace it, instead of getting rid of the whole machine.

After he invented the cotton gin, Eli Whitney made the use of interchangeable parts popular in America. He built equipment that produced large numbers of identical parts quickly and at a low cost. The parts he made were used for soldiers' muskets. By the 1850s, arms makers around the world followed what became known as the American System of Manufacture. This system quickly spread to other industries and products, from sewing machines to automobiles. ⊕

PICK YOUR OWN
Cotton

Before Eli Whitney invented the cotton gin, cotton farmers had to pick seeds from cotton bolls before they could be sold at market. Now it is your turn to try your hand at picking cotton!

SUPPLIES
• • • • • • • • • • • •

❀ paper towel or newspaper

❀ white glue

❀ 8 to 10 cotton balls

❀ a handful of small seeds or nuts

1 First, spread a paper towel or newspaper over your workspace to protect it.

2 Glue the cotton balls together into one big boll of cotton. Let it dry.

3 Insert a seed or nut into the cotton. You may need to pull some of the cotton fibers to push the seed deeper into the ball.

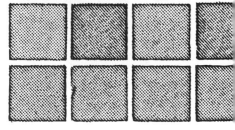

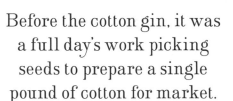
DID YOU KNOW?

Before the cotton gin, it was a full day's work picking seeds to prepare a single pound of cotton for market.

4 Repeat until all seeds are inserted.

5 Now imagine that you are picking and cleaning cotton. Pull each seed out. Turn the cotton ball over to make sure you have not missed any. See how long it takes you to clean a small piece of cotton. It is not surprising that Whitney's cotton gin was a success!

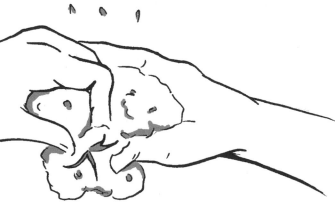

WORK ON AN
Assembly Line

Before factories, people built products from start to finish by themselves. In a factory, the building of products is broken down into many steps. A different person performs each step. To make a table, one person might make the legs, while another cuts the tabletop. Yet another person puts the parts together. This assembly-line system is faster than having one person do everything to make the product. In this project, you can recruit a few friends or family members to create your own assembly line!

1 First, see how long it takes each person in your group to create the dress alone:

* *Start the timer and begin work.*

* *Cut out the pattern with scissors*

* *Using the pattern, cut out pieces of fabric for the dress*

* *Sew the arms to the dress body*

* *Sew the skirt to the dress body*

* *Sew three buttons down the front of the dress body.*

* *Decorate the dress by sewing a piece of lace trim at the collar and at the bottom hem.*

* *See how long it takes for your group to create several dresses.*

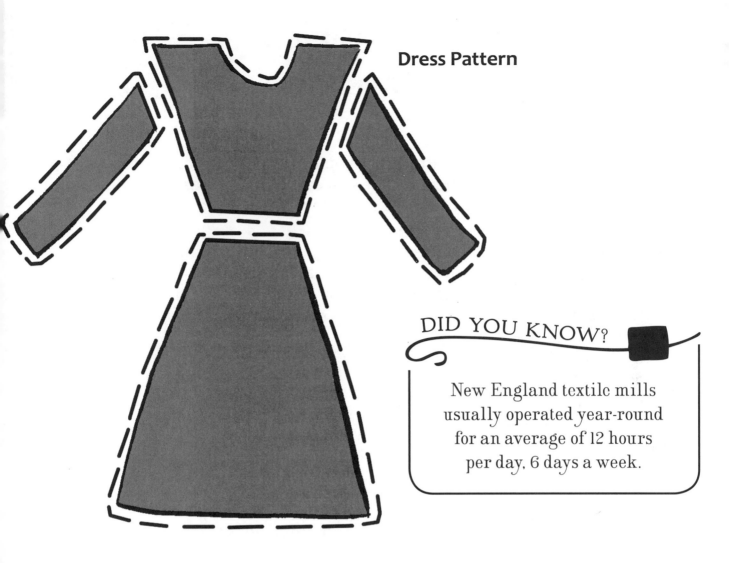

Dress Pattern

> ## DID YOU KNOW?
>
> New England textile mills usually operated year-round for an average of 12 hours per day, 6 days a week.

2 Next you will create the same number of dresses using a factory assembly line. Assign each task to a different person. One person should also inspect the final product. If you do not have enough people for each task, combine tasks (1 and 2, 3 and 4, etc.)

* *Start the clock and begin work.*

* *See how long it takes your assembly line to complete the same number of dresses as before.*

Which method produced dresses faster?

What improvements could you make on the assembly line to make it run faster?

BECOME AN
Inventor

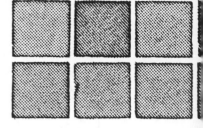

Inventors like Eli Whitney came up with new ideas or improved the way objects worked. Have you ever had any ideas for a new product or a way to make something work more efficiently?

SUPPLIES

• • • • • • • • • • • • •

⊛ a piece of paper

⊛ pen or pencil

⊛ computer with Internet access

1 Think about things you use at home or at school. Can you think of a way to make one of these things work better? Or perhaps you can think of an entirely new thing that can make life easier.

2 On a piece of paper, write down some notes about your idea. Sketch a drawing of what it would look like. Include details about how it would look, what materials you would need to build it, and how it would work. Can you make a model of your invention?

3 Once you have your invention idea down on paper, investigate to make sure no one else has patented your invention. Look in catalogs, stores, and online.

4 If you were an inventor, you might want to file for a patent to stop others from stealing your idea. You don't need a finished invention for a patent; you can submit a patent application based on an idea. Information on how to apply for a patent is on the U.S. Patent Office Web site: www.uspto.gov. Inventors under the age of 18 need a parent or guardian to apply for the patent for you. Some patents are expensive and can cost several thousand dollars to file and maintain.

CHAPTER THREE

Birth of the Labor Union

During the Industrial Revolution, many people took factory jobs hoping for a better life. But they quickly discovered that factories were grim places to work. A typical working day was 12 to 16 hours long. In the winter, factories were very cold because they didn't have heat. In the summer, factories were very hot and humid. The work itself was usually boring as workers repeated the same task all day long.

Factory work was also dangerous. Factories had few windows for fresh air, so pollution filled the mills. Poor lighting led to many accidents. Machines without safety devices crushed workers' hands and arms. Metalworkers handled **toxic** materials every day.

FOR MANY, POOR WORKING CONDITIONS LED TO HEALTH PROBLEMS.

WORDS TO KNOW

toxic: poisonous.

regulation: an official rule or order.

blacklisted: put on a list of people who are considered untrustworthy or not suitable.

Textile workers developed lung diseases from breathing cotton dust and fiber. Children developed knock-knees or bowlegs from standing all day.

If workers got hurt or sick on the job, they were responsible for getting themselves to the hospital or doctor and paying for any medical treatment. While workers recovered, they did not earn wages. If they took too long getting back to work, another worker might take their job.

DID YOU KNOW?

The average factory worker in the mid 1800s had less free time than slaves on southern plantations.

Factory owners could treat workers this way because there were no **regulations** to protect employees. They didn't spend money to make a factory safer because it meant less profits. As long as there were enough people willing to work, owners had no reason to change.

If workers complained, they risked being **blacklisted**. An employee who was blacklisted became known as a troublemaker. No employer in town would hire him. As a result, many workers kept quiet about conditions because they feared losing their jobs.

GUILDS

Before the Industrial Revolution, skilled **artisans** created a variety of fine goods, from shoes and cloth to furniture. They sold these high-quality goods in small workshops in local markets.

The artisans banded together to form **guilds**. Each type of craft had its own guild: bakers, shoemakers, or carpenters, for example. The guild made sure that its members produced high-quality goods and were treated fairly. To keep quality high, guilds arranged for the training of new crafters. A boy lived with a master as an apprentice where he learned a craft. For three to eleven years, the boy performed small chores and learned the trade. After he completed his **apprenticeship**, the young man became a day worker for the master. To become a master himself, the young man had to show his skill and create a masterpiece approved by the guild.

WORDS TO KNOW

artisan: someone who is skilled at a craft.

guild: a group of people with a common interest or goal.

apprenticeship: the time served as an apprentice.

monopoly: when a person or group controls a product or industry.

The guilds were powerful in the towns. They often maintained a **monopoly** on a craft. Their laws controlled competition, fixed prices and wages, and set sales hours. If a new artisan came to town, he could not sell goods until he joined the guild and paid fees to belong. ⊕

GROWTH OF CITIES

As factories and mills spread across America, people moved away from the country to live in cities. Immigrants coming to America often settled in cities because that's where the work was.

At first, most people lived within walking distance of their factory jobs. As cities such as Philadelphia and New York became larger, fewer people could live close enough to walk to work. Public transportation, in the form of horse-drawn buses, became popular.

The poor often lived near the downtown districts, in the oldest parts of the city. Middle-class dwellers lived in neat row homes or new apartment buildings farther out. The wealthy often lived even farther away, in large homes with lawns and trees.

Cities sparkled with the wealth of industry. Luxurious stores and magnificent town halls lined well-paved roads. City residents could purchase a wide selection of goods from specialty shops.

Despite their advantages, industrial cities also had a dark side. Away from the fancy streets where the rich lived and shopped, the working class lived crowded together in badly built houses and tiny apartments. In the cold, damp rooms, diseases such as rheumatism, bronchitis, anemia, rickets, and tuberculosis were common. Unsanitary conditions polluted local drinking water. At one point it was estimated that an Irish immigrant could expect to work only 14 years in Boston before poor conditions led to his death. ⊕

– – Beginning of the American Labor Movement – –

WORDS TO KNOW

strike: when everyone walks off the job.

protest: to object to something, often in public.

In the 1830s, some workers decided to do something about the poor working conditions and formed a labor union. A labor union is a group of workers who bargain with factory owners for better wages and safer working conditions. If management ignores the union's demands, the union can call a **strike**. Sometimes these workers **protested** outside the company.

Without employees working, factories cannot produce goods and make money. This gets the owners' attention quickly. During the Industrial Revolution, unions became popular, growing in both number of members and power. In some cases, striking workers convinced owners to agree to their demands. In other cases, the strikes did not work.

THERE WERE SOMETIMES VIOLENT FIGHTS, AND PEOPLE WERE INJURED AND EVEN KILLED.

– – – – – Lynn Shoe Workers Strike – – – – –

One of the first large union strikes occurred in Lynn, Massachusetts. The introduction of new technology enabled shoe factories to make shoes faster than ever. As shoe companies tried to outsell each other, they slashed prices. To keep profit levels up, company owners cut the wages of shoemakers.

IN SOME LYNN FACTORIES, MEN WHO WERE SHOEMAKERS MADE AS LITTLE AS 50 CENTS A DAY, AND WOMEN EVEN LESS! FED UP, THE SHOEMAKERS JOINED TOGETHER AND DEMANDED BETTER WAGES. WHEN OWNERS REJECTED THEIR DEMANDS, THE UNION CALLED A STRIKE.

WORDS TO KNOW

negotiate: to discuss and reach an agreement.

In February 1860, several thousand shoe workers left their jobs and paraded down the streets of Lynn. Within a week, the strike spread throughout New England. More than 20,000 shoemakers joined the strike. From February through March, the union members refused to work. They organized the largest workers' protest the country had ever seen. Still, factory owners refused to **negotiate**. Instead, they hired out-of-town laborers. By April, many shoemakers went back to work, without an agreement, ending the strike.

– – – The Great Railroad Strike of 1877 – – –

In the summer of 1877, the United States was in the middle of a long economic depression. Like many other companies, the Baltimore & Ohio (B&O) Railroad announced wage cuts for employees. Angry over a second round of lowered wages, many B&O railroad workers refused to work. The strike quickly spread to other railroads.

MORE THAN 100,000 RAILROAD WORKERS IN 14 STATES WALKED OFF THEIR JOBS.

For a few weeks, the country's rail traffic was frozen. In Baltimore, **riots** destroyed railroad yards, track, and railcars. In Philadelphia, angry mobs set fire to buildings, equipment, and engines.

In response, 10 state governors called in thousands of **militia** to re-open rail traffic. The disagreements between workers and militia quickly turned bloody. In Pittsburgh, citizens threw stones at state militia. The militia fired into the crowd, killing 20 people and wounding many others. By the time train service resumed, more than 100 people had been killed and 5 million dollars of railroad property had been destroyed. Despite the turmoil, many railroad workers returned to their jobs without a wage increase.

WORDS TO KNOW

riot: a gathering of people protesting something, which gets out of control and violent.

militia: a group of citizens who are trained to fight but who only serve in time of emergency.

WORDS TO KNOW

picket lines: people with signs standing outside to protest. Sometimes they prevented people from entering factories.

unskilled job: work that does not need much training or education.

— — — — Owners Retaliate — — — —

Factory owners were unhappy with the growing power of unions. Owners fired workers if they complained about long hours. Some owners hired private detectives to spy on unions. Union leaders would be fired and then blacklisted. If a union did call a strike, the owners might just shut down the factory. With the factory idle, workers were not paid. In many cases, factory owners hired strikebreakers to cross **picket lines** and replace striking workers.

IMMIGRATION

As factory production increased each year, factory owners needed more workers. Some American factories looked for workers in Europe. They sent agents to tell people about the jobs available in America. Facing poverty and hunger at home, people from England, Ireland, Poland, and many other countries decided to take a chance on America.

Immigrants coming to America hoped for a job and a better life. Although factory conditions were hard and the pay was low, it was an improvement over what many had in Europe. Millions of immigrants settled in New York and other cities along the East Coast. Others traveled west, finding work in Pennsylvania's steel mills, West Virginia's coal mines, and Chicago's meat-packing plants. Factory owners discovered that hard-working immigrants were less likely to complain about working conditions or low wages than American workers. Before long, immigrant workers held most of the **unskilled jobs** in American industry. ⊕

CHILD LABOR

Although it's hard to imagine now, children were once an important part of the workforce. Children were small and could move quickly between factory machines. They were easy to control. Most importantly, children could be paid less than adults for the same work.

Most children worked to help support their families. Children as young as 10 years old worked 12 hours a day, six days a week. In canneries, children peeled tomatoes, snipped beans, or capped cans on an assembly line. Children as young as four worked in tobacco factories. By 1880, more than 1 million children under the age of 16 were working.

Working conditions were often dangerous for children, who were three times more likely to be injured on the job than adults. Many were also treated badly by adult supervisors. Managers might whip children they considered lazy.

Some people believed that hard work kept children out of trouble and taught them how to be responsible. Others, however, believed that it was wrong to send children to work in factories. They fought to change child labor and to improve

DID YOU KNOW?

When Samuel Slater's mill opened in Rhode Island, the oldest worker was only 12 years old.

working conditions. Some states passed laws limiting children's working hours and age, but these laws were rarely enforced. The efforts to reform child labor were not always successful until the Great Depression in the 1930s. During that time, Americans wanted scarce jobs to go to adults instead of children. ⊕

— — — — Violence Erupts in Homestead — — — —

One of the most violent clashes between a union and factory owners and managers took place on July 6, 1892 at the Homestead Steel Works near Pittsburgh, Pennsylvania. A few years earlier, the union had negotiated good wages and working conditions. But Homestead's owner, Andrew Carnegie, and his plant manager, Henry Clay Frick, were determined to lower the mill's **production costs**.

WITH CARNEGIE'S SUPPORT, FRICK DEMANDED THAT THE WORKERS PRODUCE MORE STEEL.

WORDS TO KNOW

production costs: money spent to produce goods.

disband: to break up or dissolve an organization.

Frick cut wages and declared the mill non-union. When the union refused to accept the new conditions, Frick announced that he would no longer negotiate with them. Carnegie and Frick mistakenly believed that the mill workers would **disband** the union in order to keep their jobs. Instead, they went on strike. With Carnegie's approval, Frick locked out the striking workers.

He built a fence 3 miles long (nearly 5 kilometers) and 12 feet high (3½ meters) around the Homestead plant, topped with barbed wire and searchlights. The workers called it Fort Frick. Then Frick sent for 300 agents from the Pinkerton National Detective Agency to protect the mill's property. He planned to hire strikebreakers and reopen the mill without the striking workers.

A COMMON CAUSE

The American Labor Movement arose when millions of working people joined together to fight for better working conditions. Many of the benefits that today's workers enjoy, such as eight-hour days, minimum wage laws, rules against child labor, paid holidays and vacation, and health insurance were fought for by unions during the Industrial Revolution. ⊕

Heavily armed, the Pinkerton guards arrived by river barge in early July. As the guards tried to land, approximately 10,000 strikers gathered. The two sides quickly clashed and shots rang out. The battle raged for hours. At the end of the day, the outnumbered Pinkertons eventually surrendered. Nine strikers and seven detectives were killed and many more were wounded.

With the help of 8,000 state militia, Frick's strikebreakers got the mill running again. Eventually, the strike lost momentum and ended in November 1892. Local officials arrested strike leaders and charged them with murder. The steel companies blacklisted the strike leaders. Carnegie banned the union from his company, and moved quickly to increase worker hours and lower wages.

THE HOMESTEAD STRIKE INSPIRED WORKERS, BUT IT DAMAGED THE RELATIONSHIP BETWEEN UNIONS AND MANAGEMENT FOR DECADES.

Unions Join Forces

The first unions were made up of skilled workers who did similar jobs. But workers soon realized that if a single union could influence a company, then larger groups of many unions could be even more powerful. In the mid-1860s, a group of labor unions representing both skilled and unskilled workers joined together to form the National Labor Union (NLU).

By the early 1870s, the NLU had more than 600,000 members. They **petitioned Congress** to pass labor reform laws and shorten the legal workday to eight hours.

The NLU's success was mixed. Congress passed the eight-hour workday but cut wages at the same time. Although the NLU dissolved in 1873, it made people aware of labor issues. It paved the way for other labor organizations such as the Knights of Labor and the American Federation of Labor (AFL).

WORDS TO KNOW

petition: to send a letter signed by many people asking those in power to change something.

Congress: a group of people who represent the states and make laws for the country.

tailor: someone who makes, sizes, or repairs clothing.

DID YOU KNOW?

The AFL still exists as part of the AFL-CLO, one of the largest labor unions in the country.

Knights of Labor

The Knights of Labor began in 1869 as a secret group of **tailors** who worked in the Philadelphia mills. When Terence V. Powderly took over as leader in 1879, the group grew rapidly. Unlike some unions, the Knights of Labor accepted all workers in an industry, including women and African Americans. By 1886, the group had 700,000 members.

American Federation of Labor

In 1886, a group of union leaders led by Samuel Gompers founded the American Federation of Labor. Within a year, the AFL had 500,000 members. By 1904, it grew to 1.7 million members. Unlike the Knights, the AFL did not allow unskilled workers, African Americans, or women to join in its early years.

Under Gomper's lead, the AFL became the largest labor organization in the United States. It fought for higher wages, safety and health in the workplace, the end of child labor, and protection against cheap immigrant labor. Although Gompers believed workers had the right to strike, he thought workers should try to negotiate with their bosses to reach an agreement together. He wanted strikes to be used only if negotiations failed.

THE BOMB OF HAYMARKET SQUARE

In 1886, workers at the McCormick Harvesting Machine Company in Chicago went on strike, demanding an eight-hour workday. After a confrontation between strikers and strikebreakers, police fired on the strikers. The police killed four and wounded many others. The next day, a rally to protest the police brutality took place in Chicago's Haymarket Square.

At first, the gathering was peaceful. But when policemen ordered the crowd to disburse, a pipe bomb exploded in the police ranks. Several policemen died and more than 60 people were injured. The police then fired wildly into the crowd, killing several more people.

Although there was no evidence to prove who threw the bomb, some union men from the Knights of Labor were put on trial and convicted of conspiracy to commit murder. The Illinois governor pardoned several in 1893. Many left the Knights of Labor to join the more moderate AFL. ⊕

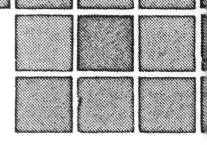

BUILD YOUR OWN
Picket Sign

When workers went on strike, they usually walked in picket lines down city streets or near companies to protest unfair conditions. Usually, workers carried signs to tell people why they were striking and what they were trying to change. Now it's your turn to create a picket sign!

SUPPLIES

- paper
- pencil
- poster board
- markers
- masking tape
- yardstick or long, wooden pole

1 First, pretend you're a factory worker. Think about why you are striking. What do you want to change? Make a list of three demands that you have for management.

2 Brainstorm and write down several short slogans or messages to communicate your demands. Pick the one that best expresses what you want to say.

3 Write your slogan in big, thick letters on a piece of poster board. Use markers to make sure it can be easily read from a distance.

4 You may decorate the poster to draw attention to your message, but be careful that your decorations do not draw attention away from your main message.

5 Use masking tape to attach the poster to a long wooden pole or yardstick. You are ready to go on strike!

Classroom Connection: Divide your class into two groups—labor and management of a shoe factory. Have each side come up with three demands (for example, work hours per day, workdays per week, number of daily breaks, wages per hour). Together, the two sides should try to negotiate an agreement so that they can avoid a strike.

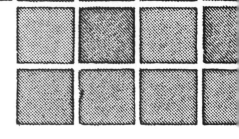

WRITE YOUR OWN
Working Song

SUPPLIES
• • • • • • • • • • • •

❂ paper

❂ pencil

During the Labor Movement, songs were used to unite people and influence how they thought about work and working people. Often these songs were set to familiar tunes so that people would find them easy to remember and join in. One song that girls in the Lowell mills sang went like this:

Oh! Isn't it a pity, such a pretty girl as I—
Should be sent to the factory to
pine away and die?
Oh! I cannot be a slave,
I will not be a slave,
For I'm so fond of liberty
That I cannot be a slave.

Try writing your own words to a popular song. Brainstorm what you want to say about work in the song. How will your song affect how people think or feel about work? You could also write a song about something that relates to you daily life, like school, friendships, or family.

1 Select a modern song to use as music. Write down your lyrics.

2 Practice and perform your song for friends and family. See if they have ideas for new songs based on their experiences.

DID YOU KNOW?

Child labor was finally outlawed in 1938 when the Fair Labor Standards Act prohibited employment of any child under age 14, except for farm work.

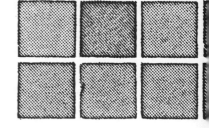

INVESTIGATE
Today's Workplace

SUPPLIES
• • • • • • • • • • • • •

❀ union and non-union adults to interview

❀ paper

❀ pencil

Workers during the Industrial Revolution often faced unfair and unsafe working conditions. What are today's working conditions like? Interview adults to find out how conditions compare. Try to find at least one adult who is not a member of a union and another who is (such as a teacher, electrician, postal worker, auto worker, or airline pilot) so you can learn why people join unions today. You might want to ask some of the following questions. Write down the answers.

* *What type of job do you have?*

* *Where do you work—an office, a factory, a store?*

* *What is it like where you work?*

* *What are the positives and negatives about your work environment?*

* *How does your job affect your life outside of work?*

* *What changes would improve your working conditions? (for example, more flexible hours, on-site daycare, more vacation time, better health care coverage, better equipment)*

* *Is there a union at your workplace? Are you a member? What issues does the union handle at your workplace?*

When you are done, look over your notes. What do you think about conditions in the workplace and the role of unions?

CHAPTER FOUR

Transportation

Before the Industrial Revolution, people traveled by foot, horse, or horse-drawn carriage. Companies **transported** raw materials and finished goods by boat or wagon. As the Industrial Revolution spread, factories produced more and more products. Moving those goods, however, was still a problem. Businessmen realized that they needed faster and cheaper ways to get their goods to more people around the country.

WORDS TO KNOW

transport: to move people and goods from one place to another.

– – Steamboats on the River – –

In the early 1800s, riverboats were one of the least expensive ways to move goods. People loaded their goods onto the boats and floated them down the river. Sending goods upstream was difficult, though, because they had to move against the **current**. Inventors realized that a steam engine could provide enough power to move a boat against a river's current.

In 1790, inventor John Fitch built a steamboat that carried passengers on the Delaware River between Philadelphia and Trenton, New Jersey. Although his steamboat worked well, people were afraid the steam engine would explode. Few wanted to ride on it. As a result, Fitch's steamboat service cost more than he collected in **fares** and he lost money.

Several years later, Robert Fulton traveled to England to study canals, engines, and the latest mechanics. At some point, Fulton turned his mind to steamboats. He studied the successes and failures of the steamboat inventors before him. He built small models and experimented with several designs. Fulton believed that if he could make a steamboat powerful and large enough, it could transport both passengers and **freight**.

After a failed experiment in Paris, Fulton built a steamboat in New York City named the *Clermont*. Most people thought Fulton's ship would not succeed. They nicknamed it Fulton's Folly. Sailboat owners felt threatened by Fulton's steamboat, and some tried to destroy it. To protect the boat, Fulton hired men to watch her day and night.

WORDS TO KNOW

current: the steady movement of water in a certain direction.

fare: the cost of traveling on a bus, subway, train, plane, boat, or other mode of transportation.

freight: goods transported by truck, train, ship, or plane.

In August 1807, a crowd of people gathered on a New York dock to stare at Fulton's strange-looking steamboat. It stretched 150 feet long (46 meters) and 13 feet wide (4 meters). It was three times larger than any other steamboat. There was a mast at each end, with small sails. A smokestack blew clouds of smoke from the deck. On the sides of the boat, paddle wheels turned.

TO THE CROWD'S AMAZEMENT, THE BOAT PULLED AWAY FROM THE DOCK.

It sailed 150 miles up the Hudson River (240 kilometers) from New York City to Albany, traveling around 5 miles (8 kilometers) per hour. Along the way, Fulton described passing many boats as if they were at anchor. Although slow by today's standards, the *Clermont* was much faster than other boats. It was also faster than traveling by land.

The *Clermont* began making regular trips between Albany and New York City. As a passenger ship, the *Clermont* was a success. Charging the same fare as other boats, the *Clermont* made the trip in an average of 36 hours, much less than the 48 hours it took a sailboat. Passengers soon crowded the *Clermont's* decks.

STRONG AS STEEL

Inventors needed strong materials to build their machines. Steel was much stronger than the iron used for steamships, but it was expensive and took a long time to make. In 1856, English inventor Henry Bessemer discovered a way to produce large quantities of strong, cheap steel. Steel quickly began to replace iron as the building material of choice. With steel, builders constructed large buildings, railroads, and bridges. ⊕

After Fulton's success, demand for steamboats skyrocketed. Within a few years, steamboats regularly steamed up and down the nation's rivers. Some transported passengers, while others transported goods. Steamboat travel was faster and cheaper than anything the nation had seen. With a steamboat, a person could travel from New Orleans to Louisville, Kentucky in about a week, a trip that had previously taken a month.

THE COST OF TRANSPORTING GOODS UPRIVER DROPPED SIGNIFICANTLY.

Before long, steamships moved from rivers to oceans. By the late 1850s, steamboats had become a popular way to cross the Atlantic Ocean between the Americas and Europe. These ships carried passengers, mail, and light freight. The trip usually took about a week.

Digging Canals

What about places in between rivers? It was still difficult to send and receive goods in these areas. To solve this problem, inventive engineers built canals to connect rivers.

One of the first great canals was the Erie Canal. This 363-mile waterway connected Lake Erie at Buffalo and the Hudson River at Albany (585 kilometers). Considered an engineering marvel, some people called it the Eighth Wonder of the World.

WORDS TO KNOW

aqueduct: a large bridge built to carry water across a valley.

Construction on the Erie Canal began in 1817. It was a risky and expensive project and many did not think it would succeed. When it was finally completed in 1825, the canal included 18 **aqueducts** over ravines and rivers. Eighty-four locks allowed the water level to be raised and lowered according to the land. The canal was just 4 feet deep (1¼ meters) and 40 feet wide (12 meters). But boats carrying 30 tons of freight (27 metric tons) could float down the canal. A 10-foot wide towpath (3 meters) on each side of the canal was built so horses, mules, and oxen could pull the boats along. This is because water in a canal does not have a current like a river.

LEVEL OF THE HUDSON RIVER

After it opened, settlers used the Erie Canal to travel west. Farmers settled the rich farmlands of Ohio, Indiana, and Illinois. With the canal, they could send their crops to markets in the East and receive manufactured goods. The canal allowed New York City to ship goods much faster than other ports. It quickly became the busiest port in America.

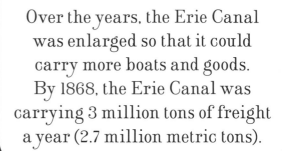

DID YOU KNOW?

Over the years, the Erie Canal was enlarged so that it could carry more boats and goods. By 1868, the Erie Canal was carrying 3 million tons of freight a year (2.7 million metric tons).

The success of the Erie Canal triggered a canal-building boom across the country. Businesses realized that canals were an inexpensive way to ships goods and reach new markets. Before the Erie Canal, cargo transported between Buffalo and New York City cost between $90 and $125 a ton. After the canal was built, shipping costs dropped to $4 per ton. By the 1840s, over 3,000 miles (4,800 kilometers) of man-made canals criss-crossed the United States.

Travel by Road

Roads were poorly maintained before the Industrial Revolution. In wet or wintry weather, they grew thick with mud and were sometimes impassable. People riding horses and wagons had to go very slowly.

In 1806, Thomas Jefferson signed **legislation** for the first **federally sponsored** highway to be built from Cumberland, Maryland, to the Ohio River. The road was known by several names: the National Road, the Cumberland Road, and the National Pike.

WORDS TO KNOW

legislation: new laws.

federally sponsored: when the government pays for something.

Work began in 1811. It was a long, backbreaking process to build the road. There were no bulldozers or trucks. Instead, men had to cut trees, clear brush, level hills, and move rocks by hand. Slowly, the road inched westward. Bridges carried the road across rivers and streams. In 1818 the road reached the Ohio River, but the project was expanded and the building continued. In 1838 the National Road arrived at its destination over 800 miles later (1,287 kilometers) in Vandalia, Illinois. The total cost of the road was almost $7 million.

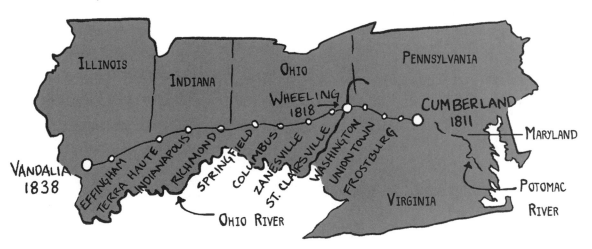

Thousands of people used the new road every year. Horse-drawn wagons pulled raw materials, animals, and goods along the National Road. Coaches carried mail and stage lines transported passengers. Factory goods could now reach new customers. Cities and towns grew along the road's path.

Next Stop: Railroads

At one time, railroads were simple wagons set on tracks and pulled by horses. But the invention of the steam engine changed things. In England, engineers built steam **locomotives** to take passenger railcars between cities. American engineers copied the British, and built short railroad lines in New England to haul lumber, stone, or other goods to waterways where workers loaded them on ships. Early railroads were generally not used for long-distance travel. As of 1830, there were only 23 miles of railroad track (37 kilometers) in the United States.

WORDS TO KNOW

locomotive: an engine used to push or pull railroad cars.

transcontinental: crossing a continent.

Then, in the mid-1800s, gold was discovered in California. The California Gold Rush drew thousands of people to the West. But it wasn't easy to get there. A wagon train from the Mississippi River to Oregon could take four to eight months. Stagecoaches had to travel along bumpy trails from the Midwest to California, and they were very expensive.

INDUSTRIAL LEADERS KNEW THAT LARGE RAILROADS COULD MOVE PEOPLE AND GOODS MUCH FASTER AND CHEAPER THAN HORSE-DRAWN WAGONS.

They took their case to Washington, DC, and convinced Congress to pay for a **transcontinental** railroad. Such a railroad, they argued, would also speed up postal delivery and could be used by the military. Congress passed the Railroad Acts of 1862 and 1864, which granted money and land to build a transcontinental railroad.

In the Midwest, the Union Pacific railroad company laid track west towards California. From California, the Central Pacific railroad company laid track east towards the Midwest. For six years, the two companies competed to lay the most track.

WORDS TO KNOW

sabotage: the planned destruction of property, or an act that interferes with work or another activity.

Building railroads was hard, dangerous work. Thousands of workers, including Irish and German immigrants, former soldiers, freed slaves, and Chinese immigrants laid track almost entirely by hand. Workers had to dynamite rock to get through mountains and across rivers. Along the way, they faced Native American attacks, **sabotage** from rival companies, buffalo herds, avalanches, floods, and dust storms.

ON MAY 10, 1869, THE TWO LINES MET AT PROMONTORY POINT, UTAH. AMERICA'S FIRST COAST-TO-COAST RAILROAD WAS COMPLETE.

The transcontinental railroad was a huge success. Passengers and freight could travel cheaply from east to west in days instead of months. Soon railroads were being built all over America. They created thousands of jobs and helped the United States economy grow. Because railroads could move freight quickly and cheaply, the cost of goods decreased. Communication between cities and towns improved as trains brought mail more quickly. The vast lands of the United States were connected as never before.

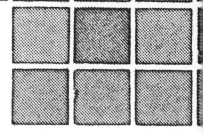

BUILD YOUR OWN
Paddlewheel Steamship

Many steamships were paddle steamers that used a paddle wheel to propel them through the water. Have an adult help you with this activity.

SUPPLIES

- 1 half-gallon milk carton
- scissors
- stapler
- duct tape
- 1 quart-sized milk carton
- white paper
- black marker
- 2 toilet paper tubes
- clear tape
- 2 craft sticks
- large cork
- 1 rubber band
- Xacto knife
- dry ice and tongs *(optional)*

1 Make the hull of your boat by cutting the larger milk container in half lengthwise. Staple the spout closed and tape it to make it watertight so your boat doesn't sink. Cover the carton design with duct tape. Keep the rest of the carton.

2 Cut the sides of the spout off the smaller milk container. Tape the remaining flaps down to create a rectangular box. This is the pilot house. You can cover the pilot house with white paper and draw or cut out windows if you want to decorate it. Put the pilot house on its side and tape it to the floor of the hull.

3 Cover the bottom of the toilet paper tubes with white paper and draw a black rim around the top to make smokestacks. Tape the tubes to each end of the pilot house.

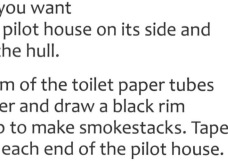

4 To make the paddle, tape one craft stick to the outside of each side of the back of the hull with duct tape. More than half of each stick should be off the end.

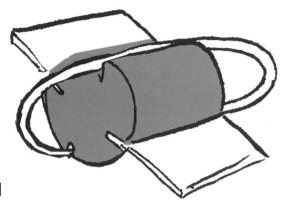

5 Have an adult help you with the Xacto knife. Take the cork and make four slits the length of the cork, equal distances apart. These will hold the paddle blades.

6 From the bottom of the leftover milk carton, cut two paddle blades the same length as the cork and wide enough to catch water. Make sure they aren't so wide that they hit the back of your boat when you attach the paddlewheel to the craft sticks.

7 Slide the blades into two opposite slits on the cork. Thread the rubber band through the two other slits. Use duct tape to keep the rubber band in the slits. Place the wheel between the craft sticks and stretch the rubber band around the outside of both sticks.

8 Place your ship in a bathtub or a pond, wind up the paddle, and watch her steam along. To have some real fun, use tongs to put dry ice in the smokestacks and make steam!

BUILD YOUR OWN
Canal Lock

A canal connects two bodies of water that may have different water levels. Boats traveling through a canal travel from one water level to another through a lock. A canal lock is a chamber shaped like a rectangle with watertight gates at each end. Inside the lock, the water level can be raised or lowered.

To travel through a lock, a boat enters one section and the gates close. Then water is added or drained to meet the level of the next section. When the water level meets the level outside the lock, the gates open to allow the boat to pass through to the new waterway. You can make a model to demonstrate this concept using a rectangular container and rice or sand.

SUPPLIES
• • • • • • • • • • • • •

⊛ sturdy cardboard

⊛ scissors

⊛ rectangular plastic container or box

⊛ rice or sand

⊛ small toy boat

1 Cut two pieces of cardboard to match the width of your box. The cardboard pieces will become your lock gates, so they must fit snugly across the bottom and sides of your box.

2 Insert your cardboard gates into your box, so that they stand perpendicular to the bottom. Your box will be divided into three sections.

3 Pour the same amount of rice or sand into the first and second sections of the box.

4 Pour rice or sand into the third section of the box. This amount should be higher or lower than the other two.

5 Place your boat in the first section. Remove the cardboard lock between the first and second sections. Move your boat into the second section and reinsert the lock behind it.

6 Now add or remove rice or sand in the second section until it matches the level of the third section. When the two sections are at the same level, remove the cardboard gate between them and "sail" your boat through.

DID YOU KNOW?

The first working railroad in the United States carried granite blocks 3 miles from the quarries in Quincy, Massachusetts, to barges on the Neponset River.

MAKE YOUR OWN
Origami Steamship

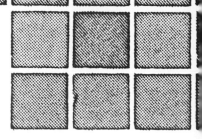

1 If you are not using origami paper, you may want to color one side of your paper to help with following the folding instructions.

2 Place the paper with the colored side down on a flat surface. Point one corner towards you so the paper makes a diamond.

3 Fold the paper in half from top corner to bottom corner. Crease and unfold. Fold in half again from left corner to right corner. Crease and unfold.

4 Fold the top corner down so that it meets the center crease.

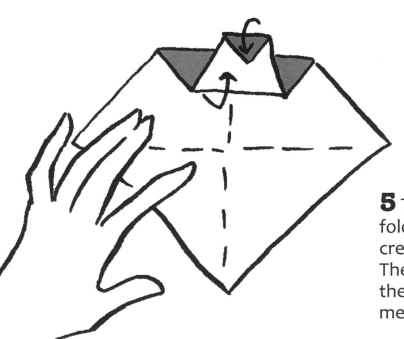

5 Take the tip you just folded and fold it up again, creating a horizontal crease about an inch from the top. The tip will be above the top edge of the paper. Fold the tip down so that it meets the top edge of the paper.

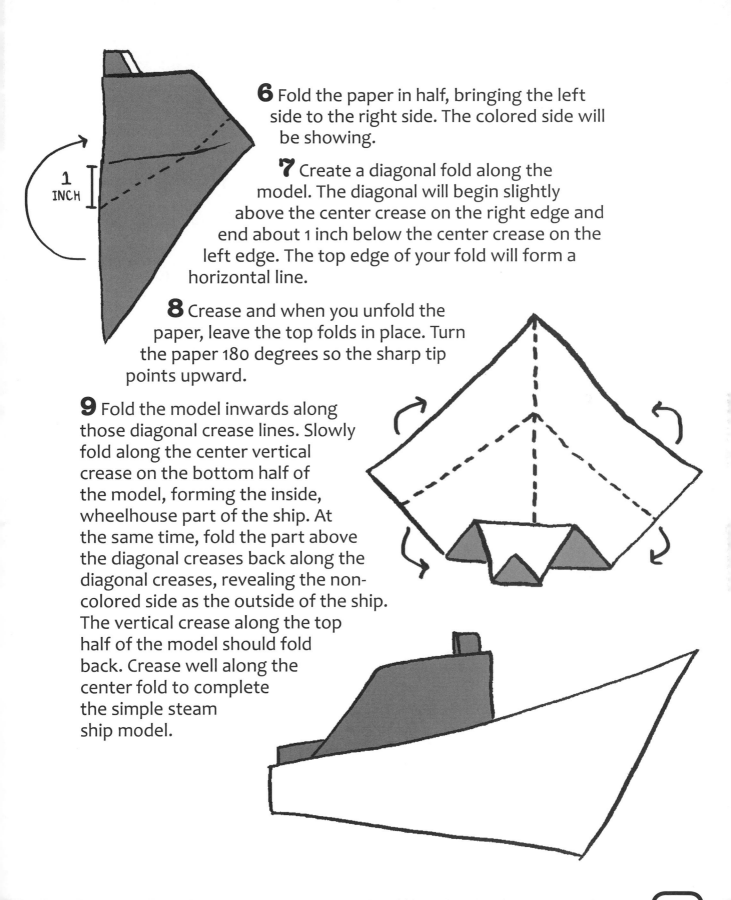

6 Fold the paper in half, bringing the left side to the right side. The colored side will be showing.

7 Create a diagonal fold along the model. The diagonal will begin slightly above the center crease on the right edge and end about 1 inch below the center crease on the left edge. The top edge of your fold will form a horizontal line.

8 Crease and when you unfold the paper, leave the top folds in place. Turn the paper 180 degrees so the sharp tip points upward.

9 Fold the model inwards along those diagonal crease lines. Slowly fold along the center vertical crease on the bottom half of the model, forming the inside, wheelhouse part of the ship. At the same time, fold the part above the diagonal creases back along the diagonal creases, revealing the non-colored side as the outside of the ship. The vertical crease along the top half of the model should fold back. Crease well along the center fold to complete the simple steam ship model.

1 INCH

CHAPTER FIVE

Communication

Thru the mid-1800s, the only way to communicate with someone who lived far away was to send them a letter. But it would take days or sometimes even weeks for a letter to reach its destination. As scientists learned about electricity, they discovered that an electrical charge could be sent from one place to another. Inventors began to experiment with the idea that electrical charges could somehow be used for communication. The result was the telegraph, a great invention that was the first step in connecting people all around the world.

— — — — Samuel Morse and the Telegraph — — — —

Samuel Morse, the inventor of the telegraph, was not a scientist. Born in Massachusetts in 1791, Morse was an artist. For years, he tried to make a living as a portrait painter and landscape artist. However, in 1832 while Morse was on a ship sailing from Europe to the United States, he had a conversation with an inventor about **electromagnetism**. After learning that an electric signal could be sent along a very long wire, Morse started thinking about using pulses of electricity to **transmit** messages.

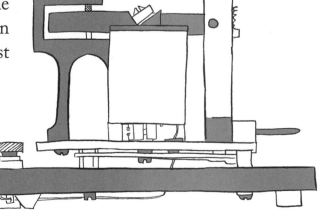

WORDS TO KNOW

electromagnetism: magnetism formed by a current of electricity.

transmit: to send or pass something from one place or person to another.

For several years, Morse worked on building a simple telegraph machine to send messages using electricity. He finally came up with a working model that used a homemade battery and two sets of wires. The sender tapped on a key using a special code Morse created. Morse code used short and long taps called "dots and dashes" to represent each letter of the message. The telegraph sent the dots and dashes as electric pulses over the wires.

A person at the receiving end translated the code and read the message. Instant communication was now possible for the first time in history.

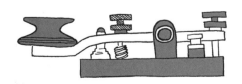

Morse demonstrated his telegraph at exhibitions and in front of businessmen and members of Congress. He hoped to find someone to give him enough money for a large test of his telegraph system. Most people did not believe that Morse's telegraph would really be able to send messages from one city to another over a thin wire.

Finally, in 1843, Congress granted Morse $30,000 to build a 30-mile telegraph line (48 kilometers) between Washington, DC, and Baltimore, Maryland.

ON MAY 24, 1844, MORSE TAPPED HIS FIRST MESSAGE: "WHAT HATH GOD WROUGHT?"

CENTENNIAL EXHIBITION

On May 10, 1876, President Ulysses S. Grant officially opened the first world's fair held in the United States. The 1876 Centennial Exposition celebrated the country's 100th anniversary. It also displayed American industrial progress.

Nearly 9 million people came to Philadelphia to experience 30,000 exhibits from 37 countries. They saw row after row of new inventions, including gas stoves, typewriters, copy machines—and Alexander Graham Bell's telephone. American inventor Thomas Edison also attended the fair and displayed new telegraph machines.

The Centennial Exhibition was a great success. Foreign visitors were impressed with the United States and its growing industrial strength. A London newspaper reported that the products of America had surpassed those of Britain. The Exhibition showed the world that America was no longer simply a nation of farmers. It had become one of the world's major industrial powers. ⊕

In 1866, the first telegraph line was laid across the Atlantic Ocean to send telegraph messages between the United States and Europe.

Morse's successful large-scale demonstration of the telegraph led to a communication revolution. Telegraph lines were built across the country. By 1854, there were 23,000 miles of telegraph wire in use (37,000 kilometers). Messages that had once taken days or weeks to deliver were now transmitted in seconds.

Although the telegraph transformed communications, it eventually fell out of use when a new invention, called the telephone, took the country by storm.

— — Alexander Graham Bell and the Telephone — —

In 1876, a young inventor displayed a strange machine at the Centennial Exhibition in Philadelphia. But few people paid attention to Alexander Graham Bell and the odd telephone he had patented a few weeks earlier.

WORDS TO KNOW

vibration: a back and forth movement.

Born in Scotland to a deaf mother, Bell became interested in the idea of reproducing sound. He knew that sound created **vibrations** in the air. Bell thought there had to be a way to create similar vibrations in an electric current. If he could do that, Bell was convinced that it would be possible to transmit sounds via electricity. To learn more, he read about and attended lectures on science and technology. Bell also hired a young mechanic, Thomas A. Watson, to help him build a working model of his idea.

Bell and Watson built a model using telegraph devices that were connected by wires. Each device had a metal strip called a reed. Sound caused the reed to vibrate, which created movement in the electrical current as it was sent over the wire. They found that different tones changed the strength of the vibration over the wire. In March 1876, Bell spoke his historic first telephone message, "Mr. Watson, come here. I want you." Watson, working in the next room, heard Bell through the wire.

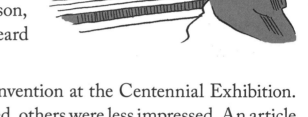

Bell then demonstrated his invention at the Centennial Exhibition. While some people were amazed, others were less impressed. An article in *The New York Times* asked, "Of what use is such an invention?"

Bell offered to sell his telephone to Western Union, the telegraph company, for $100,000. The company turned him down, believing that it had no use for an electrical toy. Determined, Bell started his own company to market his invention. He formed the Bell Telephone Company in 1877. In 1884, Bell's company opened the first long-distance telephone line, between New York and Boston.

Bell's dedication paid off as interest in his telephone quickly spread. By the 1880s, there were thousands of telephones in operation. The telephone industry created thousands of jobs across the nation.

DID YOU KNOW?

In 1878, the first telephone was installed in the White House. Alexander Graham Bell was the first person President Rutherford B. Hayes called.

By 1890, nearly 19,000 telephone operators handled calls. Thousands more worked manufacturing telephones, repairing broken telephones, and installing telephone wire. By 1900, there were 1 million telephones in operation. Bell's company owned 100 local telephone companies and handled over 2 billion calls per year.

At first, only the wealthy could afford telephones in their homes. But over time, the telephone's price fell low enough that nearly everyone could afford a phone. The telephone became the most widely used communications device in the world.

PHONE CALLS

Using an early telephone was different than it is today. There were no phone numbers or direct calls. Instead, a caller picked up the receiver and spoke to an operator. The caller told the operator who they wanted to talk to. Because the operators knew everyone in town who had a phone, they connected the caller to the right person. Eventually, numbers replaced names and callers could ask an operator to connect them to a number. Improvements such as dial telephones and automatic **switchboards** eventually replaced human operators. ⊕

MAKE YOUR OWN
Electronic Telegraph

Have an adult help you with this activity.

1 Push the fasteners partway into the cardboard about 1½ inches apart (about 4 centimeters).

2 Slide the end of the paper clip around one of the fasteners and bend upwards.

3 With scissors, gently remove about 1 inch of coating (2½ centimeters) from the ends of the copper wire pieces. You may want to make a small cut, then use your fingers to peel the rest of the coating back.

4 Twist one end of the wire tightly around one of the brass fastener heads. Twist a second wire around the other fastener head. Press both fastener heads firmly into the cardboard and secure on the other side.

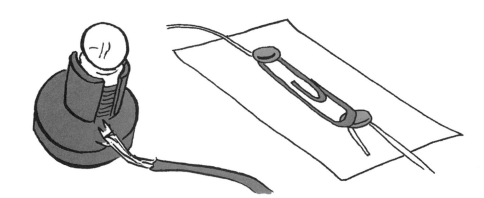

5 Screw the light bulb into its socket. Connect the wire from the fastener without the paper clip to one of the screws on the socket. Connect the wire from the other fastener to one end of the battery.

MORSE CODE

Letters			
A . -	K - . -	V . . . -	5 . . . . .
B - - . . .	L . - . .	W . - -	6 - . . . .
C - . - .	M - -	X - . . -	7 - - . . .
D - . .	N - .	Y - . - -	8 - - - . .
E .	O - - -	Z - - . .	9 - - - - .
F . . - .	P . - - .	**Numbers**	**Period**
G - - .	Q - - . -	0 - - - - -	. - . - . -
H	R . - .	1 . - - - -	**Comma**
I . .	S . . .	2 . . - - -	- - . . - -
J . - - -	T -	3 . . . - -	**Question Mark**
	U . . -	4 . . . . -	. . - - . .

6 Use the third wire to connect the battery and the other screw on the light socket.

7 The electrical circuit will be complete when you press down on the paper clip so that it touches the second fastener. It will make the bulb light up. Try tapping out a message in Morse code! A dot is a short tap and a dash is a longer tap.

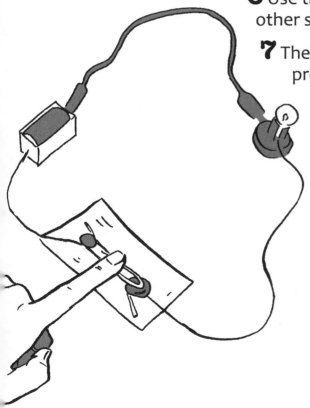

DID YOU KNOW?

In 1861, the first transcontinental telegraph line was laid by Western Union, making it the first national telegraph company.

SEND YOUR OWN
Morse Code Message

Samuel Morse developed his own code to send messages via a telegraph. Each letter or number is represented by a combination of long and short signals. Long signals are called dashes, while short signals are called dots. In this project you'll use Morse code to send your own message.

SUPPLIES

- ⊛ Morse code list *(see page 73)*
- ⊛ paper
- ⊛ pencil

1 Think of a message you want to send.

2 Translate each letter of your message into the dots and dashes of Morse code. You can write down the code on a piece of paper.

3 Using the code, tap out your message. You can clap, use a flashlight, tap on a table, or use your electric telegraph from the previous activity.

4 See if a friend can decode your message.

DID YOU KNOW?

Before the telegraph, people sent messages using flags, drums, fires, and puffs of smoke. American patriot Paul Revere used lanterns to signal the movement of British troops into Boston— one if by land, two if by sea.

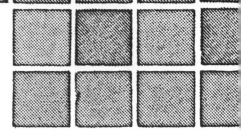

MAKE YOUR OWN
Tin Can Telephones

Here is a fun way to find out how sound travels. When someone speaks, the air vibrates. Our ears collect the vibrations and send them to our brain, which converts the vibrations into sound. On a tin can telephone, voice vibrations travel on a tight string to the other can.

SUPPLIES
• • • • • • • • • • • • •

❊ 2 metal cans, clean and dry

❊ nail and hammer

❊ 10 to 12 feet of a small diameter string, such as kite or nylon string (3 to 3½ meters)

1 Ask an adult to help you punch a small hole in the bottom of each can. The hole should be just large enough for the string to thread through it.

2 Insert one end of the string into the hole in one can. Tie some knots in the end of the string to anchor it inside the can.

3 Repeat with the other end of the string and the other can.

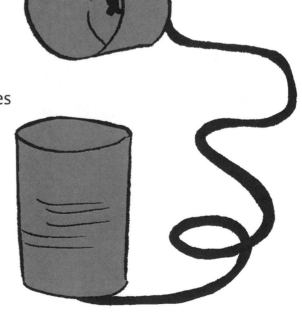

4 Have two people hold the cans, moving apart so that the string stretches tight between them. As one person talks into the can, the sound sends vibrations through the tightened string. The other person, holding the can to his or her ear, should be able to hear what was said.

CHAPTER SIX

Thomas Edison and Electricity

Thomas Alva Edison was one of the greatest inventors of all time, and a key figure in the Industrial Revolution. Best known for the light bulb and electricity, Edison was an inventor at heart. Over his lifetime, he received more than 1,000 patents, many more than any other American inventor. Some of Edison's best known inventions include the **phonograph**, the storage battery, and motion picture equipment. His inventions and innovations forever changed the way people live.

WORDS TO KNOW

phonograph: a machine that picks up and reproduces the sounds that have been recorded in the grooves cut into a record.

physics: the study of the universe and how its forces interact with each other.

The Early Years

Thomas Edison was born in Ohio on February 11, 1847. From the start, young Thomas was full of questions. He constantly wanted to know how the things around him worked. In 1854, Edison's family moved to Port Huron, Michigan, where he entered school. Edison's constant questioning often annoyed his teachers and led to punishment. After a few months, Edison's mother took him out of school and taught him at home. She exposed him to **physics**, chemistry, and other sciences. Fascinated by science, Edison soon set up his own home laboratory and began performing his own experiments.

To pay for his experiments, Edison took a job as a newsboy on the railroad that ran between Port Huron and Detroit, Michigan. He sold newspapers and candy to passengers. He was so captivated by science that he set up a laboratory in the baggage car of the train where he conducted experiments in his free time. He also learned how to operate a telegraph.

By the time he was 16, Edison was skilled enough to get a job as a telegraph operator. He traveled the country for five years, working in different cities. During this time, Edison read and studied scientific journals and texts. He dreamed of being an inventor, and spent much of his paycheck on gadgets and chemicals for his experiments.

DID YOU KNOW?

When he was around 12, Edison started losing his hearing. Although he was not completely deaf, he said that being hard of hearing made it easier for him to concentrate on his experiments.

In 1868, Edison decided to devote himself to his inventions. He received his first patent in 1869 for an electric vote recorder, a machine that electronically recorded voice votes taken in an elected body such as Congress. Although the invention worked well, no one wanted to buy it. Edison decided that from then on he would only work on inventions that he believed people would want.

Edison then headed to New York City, where he invented his first commercially successful machine, the Universal Stock Printer. He also came up with new ways to improve the telegraph. Edison was paid $40,000 for these inventions. At the time, this was a small fortune for the young inventor!

MENLO PARK

In 1876, Edison built a large invention workshop in Menlo Park, New Jersey. He set up the workshop with enough equipment to work on any invention. Menlo Park was the first research and development laboratory in the United States. It would become a model for later facilities. In Menlo Park, Edison would do some of his greatest work. ⊕

— — — Edison Invents the Phonograph — — —

In his first two years at Menlo Park, Edison and his team patented 75 different inventions. These included an early battery-powered **mimeograph**, the first microphone, and an improved version of Alexander Graham Bell's telephone.

While Edison was working on improvements to the telephone, he stumbled upon an idea for the phonograph. He had attached a thin steel needle to the vibrating part of a telephone receiver so that he could feel the sound vibrations with his finger. He then started singing into the telephone. The vibrations of his voice made the needle prick his finger. The prick set Edison's mind turning. If he could record the needle's pricking movements, and then run the needle over the "recording," Edison believed that he could reproduce sound.

First he tested his theory on a piece of waxed telegraph paper. He shouted the words "Hello! Hello!" into the mouthpiece. This caused the needle to mark the paper.

WHEN HE RAN THE NEEDLE BACK OVER THE MARKINGS ON THE PAPER, EDISON HEARD A FAINT "HELLO! HELLO!"

Edison then built a machine that used a needle and a cylinder covered with tinfoil. As the cylinder was turned with a crank, the needle made markings on the tinfoil. When Edison made the machine public, it caused quite a stir. This early version of the phonograph could only record and play back about a minute of sound, but people were amazed by Edison's talking machine.

The phonograph made Edison famous around the world and inspired his nickname "The Wizard of Menlo Park." Over the next 10 years, other inventors would make improvements to the phonograph. Edison put it aside until 1888, when he improved the machine and invited famous people to record their voices. By 1900, the combined efforts of Edison and other inventors produced high-quality phonograph machines.

Lighting the World

One of the reasons Edison stopped working on the phonograph was that he was consumed with another idea—electric lighting. Light bulbs had already been invented, but they weren't useful. They were large and unwieldy, and they used tremendous amounts of electricity. Several inventors were already hard at work trying to design a better electric light bulb that could be used in homes and businesses. No one had been able to make one that burned for more than a few minutes.

At the time, gas was used to light lamps. But gas was poisonous and highly **flammable**, causing fires. Edison believed that electricity was a safer choice. If he could sell electricity like gas was sold, he knew he could make a fortune.

WORDS TO KNOW

flammable: likely to catch fire.

practical: something useful and effective in everyday situations.

carbonized: coated with carbon.

filament: a very fine wire or thread.

ON SEPTEMBER 15, 1878, EDISON ANNOUNCED THAT HE WAS JOINING THE RACE TO DEVELOP A **PRACTICAL** ELECTRIC LIGHT BULB AND A SYSTEM TO PROVIDE ELECTRIC POWER.

Edison and his Menlo Park team set to work. They built several models, but all of them failed. Despite these failures, Edison remained positive. He told his team that each failed experiment taught him something that he did not know.

For over a year, Edison searched for the right design. His big breakthrough came when he discovered that a piece of **carbonized** cotton thread could be used as a **filament** that burned for several hours. Soon, Edison improved his filament so that it lasted for much longer.

As exciting as the invention was, Edison knew that the light bulb would be of no use without an electrical system that could provide power for people's homes. Over the next year, Edison and his team invented the **components** of such a system, including sockets, switches, fuses, junction boxes, power meters, and more. They learned how to wire large numbers of lamps using a single circuit. They developed **insulation** to protect people from being **electrocuted** by power lines. Edison wired his own home and his employees' boardinghouse with electric lights.

WORDS TO KNOW

component: a part.

insulation: material that covers something in order to stop heat or electricity from escaping.

electrocuted: injured or killed with a severe electric shock.

utility: a basic service supplied to a community, such as telephone, water, gas, or electricity.

In 1882, Edison installed the first commercial electric **utility** in New York City. He directly supervised

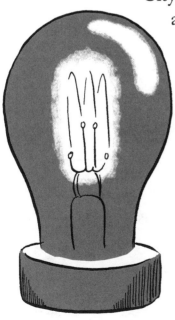

almost every aspect of the installation because few people had experience with electricity on this scale. The utility provided power to important customers like J.P. Morgan, the Stock Exchange, and several large newspapers. Edison then set up his own manufacturing company, the Edison Electric Light Company. It would make light bulbs and the parts needed for his electrical systems.

THE ELECTRIC AGE HAD BEGUN. WITHIN A FEW YEARS, TOWNS ACROSS THE COUNTRY HAD INSTALLED EDISON'S ELECTRICAL UTILITIES.

EDISON'S LIGHT BULB

A light bulb uses electricity to heat a thin strip of material called a filament. When the filament gets hot enough, it glows and produces light. Edison and his Menlo team had a very hard time finding the right kind of filament for an efficient light bulb. They tested thousands and thousands of materials without success.

Then one day while sitting in his laboratory, Edison decided to try carbonized materials for his filament. He tested the carbonized filaments of thousands of plants, including baywood, boxwood, hickory, cedar, flax, and bamboo. Eventually, Edison tested a carbonized cotton thread. The filament glowed a soft orange for fifteen hours. With further experiments and more changes he was able to make the electric light last even longer.

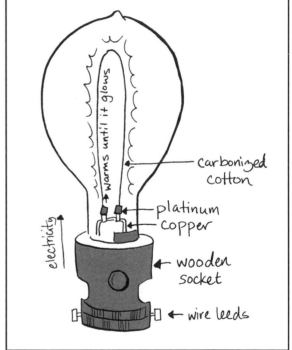

warms until it glows

electricity

carbonized cotton

platinum copper

wooden socket

← wire leeds

When asked, Edison said that developing the electric light required the greatest amount of study and the most elaborate experiments. The hard work it took to make a successful electric light inspired his famous quote, "Genius is one percent inspiration and ninety-nine percent perspiration." ⊕

WORDS TO KNOW

consolidate: to join several smaller companies into one larger company.

competitor: a person or company trying to do the same thing as another.

cultural icon: a picture, name, face, person, or other image that has meaning for a large group of people.

ingenuity: inventiveness and originality.

By 1887, there were 121 Edison power stations in the United States and several more in Europe. Edison was a partial owner in most of these local stations. Each station purchased supplies and equipment from Edison's factories. In 1889, Edison **consolidated** his electric companies to form Edison General Electric. When Edison General Electric merged with a **competitor** in 1892, it became General Electric, a large company that still exists today.

Edison's labs grew too big for his Menlo Park facilities. He decided to build an even larger complex in West Orange, New Jersey. His labs were so productive at this time that they averaged one new patent every five days!

ALWAYS EXPERIMENTING

By 1911, Edison's vast West Orange operation employed thousands of people. Edison continued experimenting with ideas and inventions until his death in 1931. During his lifetime he received 1093 patents. Along the way, this self-educated inventor became a **cultural icon** and symbol of American **ingenuity**. Although he did not invent the first light bulb, he will always be remembered for his contributions to the electric industry. In 1928, Congress presented Edison with a special Medal of Honor to recognize his lifetime of achievement. ⊕

Motion Pictures

In the late 1880s, Edison turned his attention to another invention—the motion picture. He said that he wanted to develop something that did for the eye what the phonograph did for the ear.

After several years, Edison finally succeeded in developing a workable motion picture machine called the kinetoscope. First Edison placed photographs on a long strip of film. The kinetoscope then passed the film through the field of a magnifying glass. As the viewer looked through the lens at the top of the machine, the photographs appeared to move.

When Edison demonstrated his kinetoscope at the Chicago World's Fair in 1893, it gained a lot of attention. After that, people stood in line outside kinetoscope parlors for a chance to watch short movies through a peephole viewer. Edison even produced one of the first moving pictures, *The Great Train Robbery*. Many people became interested in motion picture technology and worked to improve his early design.

CHARGE A
Light Bulb

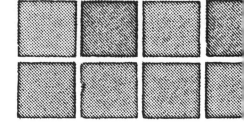

Try this easy experiment to charge a light bulb. When you rub a balloon on your hair, it builds up an electrical charge. When you hold the charged balloon close to a light bulb, the electricity jumps from the balloon to the light bulb. Have an adult supervise this activity.

SUPPLIES
• • • • • • • • • • • •

❂ fluorescent light bulb

❂ balloon

1 Blow up your balloon and turn off the lights.

2 Rub the balloon on your hair for several seconds to build up a static electricity charge.

3 Hold the balloon near the end of the light bulb and watch as the bulb lights.

WAR OF CURRENTS

Edison's electrical systems used something called direct current. The drawback to this system was that it could only send electricity about a mile away (1½ kilometers). Any farther and light bulbs grew dim. One of Edison's competitors, George Westinghouse, developed a new system that used high-voltage alternating current. This technology could send electricity hundreds of miles with little power loss. Edison, however, stubbornly resisted using alternating current. A war of the currents erupted, but in the end Westinghouse's alternating current emerged as the winner. ⊕

MAKE YOUR OWN
Homemade Battery

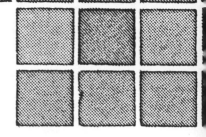

SUPPLIES

- lemon
- copper penny *(minted before 1982)*
- silver dime
- old toothbrush
- soap and water
- knife

One of Edison's most profitable inventions was the storage battery. Batteries are made from two different metals suspended in an acidic liquid. In this experiment, the lemon juice is the acidic liquid and the coins are the metals. Have an adult help you with this activity.

1 Press down on the lemon and roll it around a few times on a counter to get the juices flowing.

2 Clean a penny and dime with soap and water using an old toothbrush.

3 Ask an adult to cut 2 parallel slits very close together in the lemon, about a finger width apart.

4 Insert the penny in one slit and the dime in the other slit. Be sure the coins do not touch each other.

5 Touch both coins with your tongue at the same time. What happens? You should feel a slight tingle of electricity.

DID YOU KNOW?

In the 1880s, electrical engineer Nicholas Tesla perfected the principles of alternating current. The electric coil, or the Tesla coil, keeps the current moving steadily on the power lines that supply our homes.

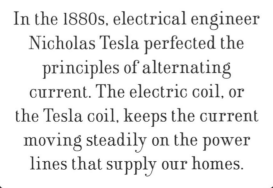

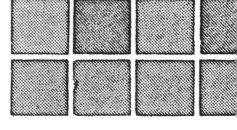

MAKE YOUR OWN
Electromagnet

- iron nail, about 3 inches long (7½ centimeters)
- 3 feet of thinly coated copper wire (about 1 meter)
- D battery
- tape or a rubber band
- paperclips

Magnets that run on electricity and can be turned on and off are called electromagnets. In this experiment, the electricity flowing through the wire makes the nail attract certain metals. An adult should supervise this activity.

1 Wrap the copper wire around and around the nail, leaving about 8 inches of wire loose at both ends (20 centimeters). Try not to overlap the wire.

2 Remove about an inch of the plastic coating from both ends of the wire (2½ centimeters).

3 Attach one end of the wire to one end of the battery and the other end of the wire to the other end of the battery. You can use tape or a rubber band to hold them in place.

4 Put the tip of the nail near a few paper clips and see how many you can pick up!

5 When you have finished experimenting, disconnect the wires so you don't drain your battery.

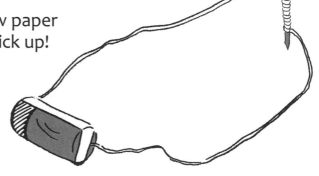

MAKE YOUR OWN
Zoetrope

A zoetrope is a cylinder with a strip of images on the inside. The zoetrope rotates the images, which are viewed through a slit. If you move many images fast enough through a single spot, your eye sees the illusion of a moving image.

SUPPLIES

* ruler
* round cardboard half-gallon ice cream container with lid, clean and dry
* scissors
* white paper, standard letter size
* tape
* black pen or marker
* black construction paper
* crayons, markers, or colored pencils
* masking tape
* marble or large glass bead

1 Measure about 4 inches from the bottom of the ice cream container (10 centimeters). Trim the top off with scissors.

2 Fold a piece of white paper into thirds lengthwise, then cut into strips.

3 Tape two strips together to create one long strip. Trim so that the strip can circle inside the ice cream container without any gaps or overlapping.

4 Using a black pen or marker, draw a series of pictures on the white strip of paper. Make sure each image is slightly different than the next.

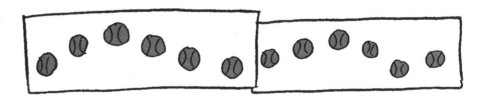

5 Cut a strip of black construction paper 6 inches wide (15 centimeters) and long enough to wrap around the outside of the ice cream container. You may have to tape two pieces together to make it long enough.

6 Tape the black strip around the outside of the ice cream container. Cut 2-inch-long slits (5 centimeters) that are about ¼ inch wide (½ centimeter). Make sure the slits are evenly spaced.

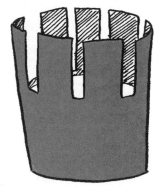

7 Tape the illustrated white paper inside the container near the bottom, with the illustrations between the slits.

8 To make the spinner, take the ice cream container's lid and make a hole in the center. The hole should be slightly bigger than the diameter of your marble or glass bead. Cover the hole with masking tape on the outside of the lid.

9 Make a few small cuts in the tape, from the center moving outward, to form an "x." Push the marble halfway through the hole so that it is held in place by the tape. Set the bottom of your zoetrope in the lid.

10 To view your moving picture, spin the zoetrope on a hard surface and look through the slits in the black paper to the pictures on the opposite side.

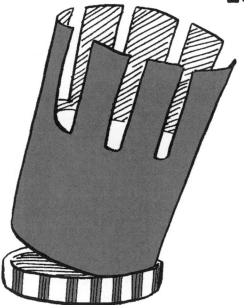

DID YOU KNOW?

Edison nicknamed his eldest two children "Dot" and "Dash" after the Morse code symbols used in telegraph messages.

MAKE YOUR OWN
Flip Book

SUPPLIES
· · · · · · · · · · · · ·

- ❀ several pieces of white paper
- ❀ scissors
- ❀ pencil, crayons, markers, or colored pencils
- ❀ stapler

A flip book is a quick and easy way to make a moving picture.

1 Cut 16 to 20 identical-sized rectangles from the white paper.

2 Draw a picture on the first piece of paper. A good idea is to draw something that moves, like a car, plane, or bouncing ball.

3 Draw the same picture on a second piece of paper, this time moving it slightly.

4 Repeat on each rectangular square, moving the image slightly each time.

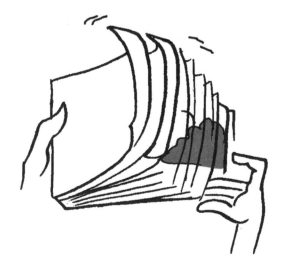

5 Staple all the rectangles together on the left hand side.

6 To show your moving picture, flip the pages quickly. Watch the image move!

CHAPTER SEVEN
Captains of Industry

Most companies were fairly small in the early years of the Industrial Revolution. Because it was so difficult to ship goods, companies usually sold their products only to people who lived nearby. But the improvements in transportation opened up a new world for companies. Steamboats and railroads carried goods to customers who lived far away. With more customers, enterprising businessmen enlarged their factories so that they could produce more goods. It was the beginning of the age of big business.

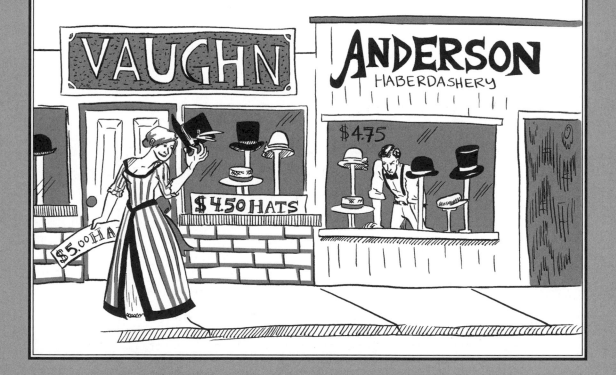

– – – – – – Age of Big Business – – – – – –

WORDS TO KNOW

financing: the amount of money that an individual or a company has.

corporation: a large company.

work ethic: a set of values that promotes hard work.

charity: an organization that helps people in need.

exploit: to benefit unfairly from someone else's work.

As companies expanded they often found themselves in competition with other companies that sold similar products. To attract buyers, companies lowered their prices. If prices dropped too low, smaller companies could not make a profit.

Larger companies with strong **financing** were better able to survive these price wars. They bought out the smaller companies. As companies grew larger they controlled more of the market. When one company controls a whole market, it can charge whatever it wants for its products because people can't get them anywhere else. This is called a monopoly. After the 1860s, monopolies dominated a large part of American business.

– – – – – – Captains of Industry – – – – – –

During the Industrial Revolution, industries such as steel, oil, and the railroads were each controlled by one huge **corporation**. The men that ran these corporations became enormously powerful and wealthy. Business leaders like Andrew Carnegie, J.P. Morgan, John D. Rockefeller, and Cornelius Vanderbilt, became known as captains of industry. They transformed the American economy with their ideas, **work ethic**, and business skills. They also used their enormous fortunes to establish and support many **charities**.

BUT AS BUSINESS OWNERS BECAME WEALTHIER, WORKERS BECAME POORER.

Workers endured horrible conditions and low wages. Some people believed that business leaders built their enormous fortunes by **exploiting** workers.

MANY BUSINESS LEADERS BECAME KNOWN AS "ROBBER BARONS."

There is still debate over the role these men and their companies played during the Industrial Revolution. Were they captains of industry that helped build the United States' industrial power? Or were they ruthless robber barons, motivated by greed and willing to step on the poor on their way to riches?

— — Andrew Carnegie and — — the Steel Industry

Andrew Carnegie was born in Dunfermline, Scotland, in 1835. Dunfermline was an important city in the textile industry, and Carnegie's father worked as a weaver. When steam-powered looms replaced men like Carnegie's father, the family struggled. Carnegie later wrote that during that time he learned what poverty meant. He would never forget that his father had to beg for work. He resolved that would never happen to him when he grew up.

The Carnegie family left Scotland, hoping to find more opportunity in America. In 1848, the family settled in Pittsburgh, and young Andrew took a job as a messenger boy in the city's telegraph office. It was there that Carnegie met Thomas A. Scott, who would later become president of the Pennsylvania Railroad. Scott took the young Carnegie under his wing and hired him as his private secretary and personal telegrapher. Under Scott's guidance, Carnegie learned the railroad business and worked his way up the ladder at the Pennsylvania Railroad.

When the Civil War began, the demand for iron skyrocketed. Carnegie saw his opportunity. He formed the Keystone Bridge Company, which worked to replace wooden bridges with stronger iron ones. Carnegie's company signed **lucrative contracts** with the railroads. Soon Carnegie was earning $50,000 a year, which was a fortune at the time.

WORDS TO KNOW

lucrative: profitable and money-making.

contract: an agreement, usually including payment of money.

DID YOU KNOW?

Andrew Carnegie was ruthless in keeping down costs. He managed his businesses by the motto "watch costs and the profits take care of themselves."

On a trip to Europe, Carnegie met Henry Bessemer, who had developed a new method for making steel from iron. Carnegie invested heavily in Bessemer's idea and built a new steel plant near Pittsburgh. He **shrewdly** named the plant after the president of the Pennsylvania Railroad. Soon after, Carnegie received a large order from the Pennsylvania Railroad for steel rails.

Over time, Carnegie bought out many other steel plants. By 1900, he controlled about 25 percent of the country's steel industry. Carnegie Steel produced more steel than all of Great Britain.

Although Carnegie believed in the right of workers to form unions, he could also be a ruthless boss. Carnegie's employees often worked long hours for low pay. One of the lowest points of his career occurred in 1892, when he supported his plant manager Henry Frick against striking steel workers. In a conflict between guards hired to protect the plant and the workers, many men were injured or killed.

Despite the tragedy, Carnegie's steel companies **prospered**. In 1901, Carnegie sold his businesses to **financier** J.P. Morgan for $480 million and became the richest man in the world. With Carnegie's companies, J.P. Morgan formed United States Steel Corporation, the largest business enterprise ever launched.

WORDS TO KNOW

shrewd: able to judge people and situations, and make good decisions.

prosper: to be successful.

financier: a person who invests large amounts of money in businesses.

DID YOU KNOW?

Large corporations that control an industry are also called trusts. President Theodore Roosevelt was called the "Trust Buster" for his efforts to put an end to powerful monopolies, like one that existed in the railroad industry.

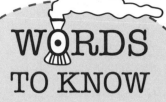

WORDS TO KNOW

philanthropy: helping others by donating money, time, or property.

trust: property or money that is held or used to benefit others.

Carnegie then devoted himself full time to **philanthropy**. In addition to funding thousands of public libraries, Carnegie established colleges, schools, and nonprofit organizations throughout the world. He also established several **trusts**. By the time he died in 1919, Carnegie had given away about $350 million. His trusts and foundations continue his charitable work to this day.

MUCKRAKERS

In the late nineteenth century, several writers tried to expose unsafe working conditions and problems such as poverty and slums. Some of the most well known were Lincoln Steffens, Ida Tarbell, and Upton Sinclair. Steffens wrote about corruption in St. Louis and Pittsburgh. Tarbell exposed Standard Oil's unfair business practices. Sinclair wrote a novel called *The Jungle*, which described the evils in Chicago's meatpacking industry. Their writings, and those of others, inspired people to call for change.

President Theodore Roosevelt supported labor reforms, but he thought that some writers went too far. He compared them to someone stirring up the mud at the bottom of a pond. This led to the nickname muckrakers. By 1910, public interest in muckraker writing began to decline. Even so, their influence on the reform movement would continue for years. ⊕

J.P. Morgan and the Finance Industry

In contrast to Andrew Carnegie's more humble beginnings, John Pierpont Morgan was the son of a successful German businessman. Born in America, he enjoyed the finest education at the University of Gottingen in Germany.

In 1857, Morgan began his career as an accountant and then moved into banking a few years later. He eventually became a partner in the New York City firm of Drexel, Morgan and Company. In 1895, the firm became J.P. Morgan and Company. Morgan used his connections with British bankers to arrange **capital** for rapidly growing American industrial corporations.

J.P. MORGAN AND COMPANY WOULD BECOME ONE OF THE MOST POWERFUL BANKING COMPANIES IN AMERICA.

In 1893, America had experienced a financial crisis and many businesses failed. Morgan had bought **distressed** businesses, especially railroads. By doing this, he helped railroads recover and made a fortune in the process. He used this method to make fortunes in other industries, including steel.

Not everyone, however, was impressed with Morgan's financial and business methods. In 1912, a federal committee investigated him. They believed that he was creating unfair monopolies because he combined smaller companies into one big corporation. He had control over most of America's industry, including almost all of the railroad and steel business in the country. They never found that he had done anything wrong and Morgan remained a giant in American banking and finance until he died in 1913. A great collector of books and art, he donated many items to New York City's museums and public libraries.

— — — John D. Rockefeller — — — and Standard Oil

John D. Rockefeller always had a nose for business. As a kid, he bought large bags of candy, divided them up, and sold them to his siblings for a profit. He was born in Richford, New York, and later moved with his family to Cleveland, Ohio, where he graduated from high school and went right to work. As soon as he could, Rockefeller started his own business in the farming industry.

Then Rockefeller decided to invest in the booming oil industry. The first successful oil well had been drilled in nearby western Pennsylvania in 1859. Rockefeller borrowed a lot of money and built his first **oil refinery** in 1863 with some partners. The company was a success and continued to grow.

WORDS TO KNOW

oil refinery: where oil from the ground is turned into useful products like gasoline.

In 1870, he and several partners formed the Standard Oil Company. As president, Rockefeller began buying up Cleveland oil refineries. He bought more than 20 companies. If a company did not want to sell to Rockefeller, he drove them out of business by selling his oil for a much cheaper price than his competitors could charge.

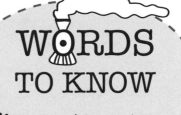

WORDS TO KNOW

suit: a complaint against someone in a court of law.

After gaining control of the Clevelend market, Rockefeller set his sights on major oil refineries across the country. He bought about 100 refineries. By 1880, Standard Oil controlled about 90 percent of the United States oil industry.

ALONG THE WAY, JOHN D. ROCKEFELLER BUILT ONE OF THE GREATEST FORTUNES IN AMERICA.

DID YOU KNOW?

Before his death in 1937, Rockefeller had spent much of his time and money on charitable causes. He established the University of Chicago, funded the Rockefeller Institute for Medical Research, and established the Rockefeller Foundation.

The government began to take notice of Standard Oil's control over the oil industry. They charged the company with having an unfair monopoly and filed **suit** against Rockefeller and Standard Oil. Eventually, the case reached the United States Supreme Court and in 1911, Standard Oil was ordered to break up.

Rockefeller had already retired from the company in 1895, long before Standard Oil split into 34 different oil companies. His fortune was estimated to be about $900 million dollars, making him one of the wealthiest men in the world.

GEORGE EASTMAN

In 1878, a young man named George Eastman wanted to take pictures while on vacation. At the time, photography needed quite a bit of equipment. Eastman had to pack a camera as big as a microwave oven, a heavy tripod, fragile glass plates, a plate holder, chemicals to develop pictures, and a tent to use as a darkroom.

Eastman was frustrated by the complicated process of spreading photographic liquid on the plates and developing them before they dried out. He began to study how to make photography easier and more enjoyable for the average person. After experimenting in his mother's kitchen for three years, Eastman developed a way to coat glass plates with a gelatin mixture. After the gelatin dried, the plate could be used for long periods, even if it was exposed to light.

In 1880, Eastman started a company to make and market his dry photographic plates. Because he loved the letter K, he chose the name Kodak for his company. In 1888, he introduced the Number One Kodak Camera for $25. After the user took pictures, they sent the camera back to Kodak, which developed and printed the pictures, put new film in the camera, and returned it all to the owner. In 1900, Kodak introduced the Brownie camera for $1 that was so easy even kids could use it.

Eastman's inventions opened the world of photography to the average person. Anyone could take pictures with a handheld camera by simply pressing a button. Kodak grew into a worldwide corporation. It also earned Eastman a fortune and made him one of America's leading industrialists. Today, the Kodak name and company are still known around the world. ⊕

— — Cornelius Vanderbilt and Transportation — —

Cornelius Vanderbilt was born into a poor family on Staten Island, New York. He quit school when he was 11 to work with his father in boating. By age 16, Vanderbilt started his own passenger ferry business, transporting people and cargo around New York harbor. During the war of 1812, he added several boats and landed a government contract to deliver supplies throughout the area.

In 1818, Vanderbilt left his ferry business and took a job with a steamship company. For the next decade, Vanderbilt learned the steamship business and saved his money. In 1829, he started his own company.

During the 1830s, Vanderbilt built his company into the main steamship line on the Hudson River. His low prices and comfortable ships attracted customers. Then he turned his attention to expanding along the coast.

BY THE 1840S, VANDERBILT OPERATED MORE THAN 100 STEAMBOATS.

In 1857, Vanderbilt entered the railroad business. He gained control of several railroads by purchasing and consolidating lines. He also established the first rail link between New York and Chicago. During the 1870s, Vanderbilt began construction on New York City's Grand Central Terminal, providing jobs to thousands. During his lifetime, Vanderbilt amassed a fortune of $100 million.

A Mixed Legacy

Men like Carnegie, Morgan, Rockefeller, and Vanderbilt created monopolies and controlled entire industries. They also dramatically lowered prices by controlling costs and increasing efficiencies. Because of these men, steel, transportation, and oil became cheaper than ever. American factories and businesses took advantage of these low prices. The American economy grew at a rapid rate.

At the same time, working conditions worsened. As a result, unions grew more popular and strikes increased. People across the country wanted the government to control the power of large corporations.

DID YOU KNOW?

At first, the government did not regulate big businesses. But many people thought that one company should not be able to control an entire industry. In 1890, Congress passed the Sherman Antitrust Act to limit the power of big business.

BUSINESS INTEGRATION

During the Industrial Revolution, companies began using horizontal and vertical integration to grow into major corporations.

Vertical integration happens when a company buys its suppliers or buyers. Rockefeller's Standard Oil owned companies that drilled for oil, refined crude oil, and transported the refined oil products to retail stores.

When a business buys companies that offer similar products or services, it is called horizontal integration. Carnegie Steel bought many companies that made iron goods. This horizontal integration enabled Carnegie to offer a wider variety of products. ⊕

MAKE YOUR OWN
Pinhole Camera

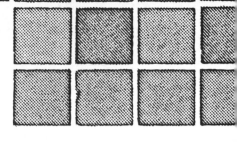

SUPPLIES
• • • • • • • • • • • • •

- ❂ empty round cardboard canister, like the kind used for oatmeal
- ❂ push pin
- ❂ pencil
- ❂ wax paper
- ❂ rubber band or tape
- ❂ dark room with a lamp
- ❂ blanket

The earliest cameras used pinhole technology to transfer a scene onto a small piece of film. In this project, you'll see how pinhole technology works.

1 Punch a hole in the center of the bottom of your cardboard canister. If the bottom of your canister is thick, use a push pin to start the hole, then finish with a pencil.

2 Place a piece of wax paper over the open end of the canister. Use a rubber band or tape to secure it in place.

3 Take your camera into a dim room with a brightly lit object like a lamp. Place the blanket over your head and the camera. Face the wax paper side towards you. Hold the camera at arm's length and let only the pinhole end stick out from under the blanket.

4 Point the camera at the lamp. You should see an image of the lamp on the wax paper. The image will appear backward and upside down.

In early cameras, the lens formed the same backward, upside-down image.

CHAPTER EIGHT

Moving Into the Twentieth Century

As the 1800s ended, American cities swelled with workers and industry. City streets were filled with carriages, trolleys, and horses. Department stores offered a wide variety of products and vendors sold goods and food along the streets. The skylines of cities changed as steel-frame skyscrapers sprung up in places like New York and Chicago.

Despite the excitement and activity in America's cities, there were also growing problems. Factories belched smoke and pollution into the air and water. Working-class families were often crowded into tiny apartments called **tenements**. In some cities, stray pigs and dogs roamed the streets. Disease was common in such conditions. Dirty drinking water spread deadly diseases like cholera. Many people died as a result of these living conditions.

WORDS TO KNOW

tenement: a run-down apartment building, especially one that is crowded and in a poor part of a city.

suburb: an area on or close to the outer edge of a city, usually made up of homes with few businesses.

— — — The Middle Class — — —

Somewhere between the fantastically rich and the desperately poor, a new American middle class emerged. They usually held good-paying jobs, such as factory managers or small business owners. While not rich, the middle class earned enough money to allow them to live better than their parents had lived.

Looking to escape the dirty, crowded cities, middle-class Americans often settled outside city limits. These areas became known as **suburbs**. The new middle class earned enough money to buy things they wanted, instead of just what they needed. At the same time, new products made household work easier. Sewing machines, electric irons, and washing machines became popular with middle-class families. Refrigerators helped keep food fresh and prevented disease.

Henry Ford and the Automobile

Middle-class life was also dramatically transformed by one of the greatest inventions of the twentieth century—the automobile. Before the automobile, most Americans still walked where they needed to go. Some rode bicycles or horses, or traveled in horse-drawn carriages.

FOR YEARS, INVENTORS TINKERED WITH THE IDEA OF A PERSONAL AUTOMOBILE.

An automobile would need a small but reliable power source. It would also need ways to start, stop, and steer. Development was a long, slow process.

WORDS TO KNOW

combustion: burning fuel to produce energy.

prototype: the first model of something new.

In the 1890s, some inventors started building cars with the newly developed internal **combustion** engine. These early cars had a one-cylinder engine with a chain drive that turned wooden carriage wheels. Drivers steered the open cars with a lever.

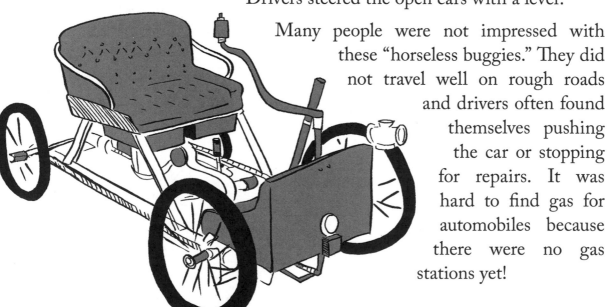

Many people were not impressed with these "horseless buggies." They did not travel well on rough roads and drivers often found themselves pushing the car or stopping for repairs. It was hard to find gas for automobiles because there were no gas stations yet!

INTERNAL COMBUSTION ENGINE

One of the biggest problems in building a car was finding a power source. Some inventors tried steam. Others experimented with electricity. German inventor Wilhelm Gottlieb Daimler is credited with inventing the first practical internal-combustion engine in 1885. It used gasoline as fuel. Daimler's engine revolutionized car design because it was lightweight, small, and fast. It would become the **prototype** for the modern gas engine. ⊕

Cars were also expensive so only the very wealthy could afford them. In Detroit, a young mechanic named Henry Ford believed that automobiles could be built at a price the average American could afford.

DID YOU KNOW?

Some people considered Ford's Quadricycle a nuisance because it made a lot of noise, scared horses, and blocked traffic.

Ford set up a workshop in a shed beside his house, where he tested and built his automobile models. In 1893, Ford's first automobile, the Quadricycle, was ready. It looked like a buggy with four rubber bicycle wheels. According to Ford, his car became quite an attraction in Detroit. Whenever he left the automobile alone for a minute, a curious person would try to run it. Eventually Ford started chaining the car to a lamppost whenever he had to leave it.

WORDS TO KNOW

masses: most of the people.

conveyor: a moving belt that carries objects from one place to another in a factory.

Over the next few years, Ford worked to improve his automobile. Using $28,000 from investors, Ford started the Ford Motor Company in 1903. At first, the company produced only a few cars a day. But Ford did not give up his dream of producing inexpensive cars for the **masses**. He said that a car needed to be powerful enough for American roads and capable of carrying its passengers anywhere that a horse-drawn vehicle could go.

In 1908, Ford introduced his Model T car. Easy to operate, maintain, and handle on rough roads, it immediately became a huge success. Ford easily sold all that he could make.

BY 1917, HALF OF ALL CARS IN AMERICA WERE MODEL TS.

At first, the Model T sold for $850. Ford and his engineers still searched for a way to increase production and lower costs. Meanwhile, he opened a larger factory at Highland Park, Michigan, in 1910.

By 1913, Ford's company had developed a moving assembly line system for building automobiles. A **conveyor** belt carried parts through a line of workers. Each worker stood in one spot and added one piece to the automobile as the conveyor belt moved past. The conveyor belt was carefully timed to keep the assembly line moving smoothly. This proved to be so efficient that the time needed to assemble a complete car dropped from 150 minutes to 26.5 minutes.

The moving assembly line was revolutionary. Ford's company could make more cars for less money. Although it was exciting for management, the assembly line was incredibly boring for workers. Standing in one spot and repeating the same task over and over was tiring and dull. People did not want to work this way. Often, they quit after a few days or weeks. Ford was forced to double wages, to $5 per day. The work was still **monotonous**, but the pay was so good that jobseekers had to be turned away.

WORDS TO KNOW

monotonous: boring and repetitive.

public works: building of roads, schools, and other projects by a government for the public.

Ford's company kept growing. During the early 1920s he built a new plant in Dearborn, Michigan. At the time the massive Rouge Plant was the world's largest industrial complex. It had everything the Ford Company needed to make cars. There was a steel mill, a glass factory, and an automobile assembly line. Each step in the automobile manufacturing process took place at the Rouge Plant.

In 1929, the price of the Model T dropped to under $300. Soon half of all the cars in the entire world were Model Ts. Ford had finally realized his dream of an affordable car for the masses.

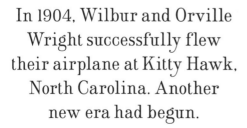

DID YOU KNOW?

In 1904, Wilbur and Orville Wright successfully flew their airplane at Kitty Hawk, North Carolina. Another new era had begun.

Ford had also jump-started the American auto industry. Steel, oil, and rubber companies grew rich selling raw materials to automakers. Roads and highways had to be built across the country. The road-building boom peaked with the Interstate Highway System, one of the greatest **public works** projects in American history.

MASS PRODUCTION

Many manufacturers quickly adopted Ford's assembly-line system of mass production to lower prices. Soon modern inventions filled American homes. Electric lamps lit rooms at night, phonographs played music, and household appliances made daily life easier.

During World War II, America turned its mass-production facilities into war factories, making airplanes and ships, as well as guns, helmets, tanks, ammunition, and combat boots. Mass production helped turn America into one of the world's greatest industrial nations. ⊕

– – Radios Broadcast Across the Nation – –

One of the most popular inventions at this time was the radio. First developed in the late 1800s, early radios were bulky, noisy, and didn't work well. But technology improved the quality of radios and made them affordable. During the 1920s, the radio craze spread across America.

The first public radio station opened in Pittsburgh in 1922. It was an immediate success. People sat around their radios and listened to everything the station **broadcast**. Soon, more radio stations opened around the country.

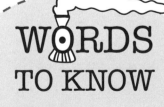

WORDS TO KNOW

broadcast: to transmit by radio or television.

Radios were a cheap and easy way to communicate information and ideas. The first broadcasts were mostly news reports, but they expanded to include concerts, sermons, and entertainment programs.

Businesses found that radio programs were a fantastic opportunity to **advertise** their products. One radio spot could reach thousands of listeners instantly. Businesses agreed to help pay for radio programs in return for advertising their products. Soon all different types of products from soap to washing machines were advertised on the radio.

WORDS TO KNOW

advertise: to make public in a positive way to increase sales.

Changing the World

From the first English textile machines to American automobiles, the Industrial Revolution brought dramatic changes to the world. In less than 200 years, it transformed how people lived and worked.

Mass production created cheaper goods that ordinary people could afford. Meanwhile, advances in transportation and communication made the world a smaller place. It was easier to visit friends and relatives who lived far away. People could talk with each other on the telephone. Later, radios and televisions brought the sights and sounds of the world into every living room. At the same time, the Industrial Revolution introduced new problems into society. Unsafe working conditions, child labor, pollution, immigrant poverty, slums, and disease were the darker side of this extraordinary time.

The spirit of invention started by the men and women of the Industrial Revolution carries forward into today. New generations of innovators create new technological marvels, from space shuttles to the Internet. It's fun to imagine what the future will bring.

RECORD YOUR OWN
Radio Program

Popular in the twentieth century, radios were a cheap and easy way to communicate information and ideas. Radio stations broadcast all types of programs from news reports to music and entertainment.

1 First, you'll have to decide what type of program you will record. Will you report the news, perform music, record an advertisement, or do a comedy skit?

2 Using pencil and paper, write a script for your radio program. Make parts for each person participating. Think of any sound effects that you can use during your program.

3 Do a trial run to rehearse your program. Remember that people listening to the radio can only hear the announcers. You must use your voice to speak clearly and show emotion.

4 Time to go on the air! Record your program. Pretend the show is live, so if you make a mistake, don't stop. Just keep moving to the next part of the show.

5 Listen to your playback. How do you rate as a radio broadcaster?

INVESTIGATE A
New Industrial Revolution

SUPPLIES
• • • • • • • • • • • •

* ❋ an adult to interview
* ❋ paper
* ❋ pencil

During the Industrial Revolution, a number of inventions and innovations transformed life in a short time. Some people believe that today's technology, including computers and the Internet, have changed life just as dramatically and quickly. Are we in the middle of a new Industrial Revolution? You can investigate and decide.

1 Interview an adult about technology in the 1970s or 1980s. How has their life changed from then until now? What are the positives and negatives about these changes? You may want to ask about the differences in:

* *telephones*

* *televisions*

* *computers and the Internet*

* *movies*

* *communication*

* *transportation*

2 Think about the changes you have learned about in your interview. Do you think they are part of a slow, unfolding process? Or are they evidence of the quick, dramatic change of a new Industrial Revolution?

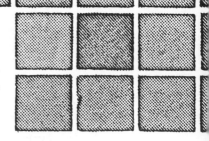

MAKE YOUR OWN
Balloon-Powered Car

Henry Ford experimented on different car models. Now it's your turn to design your own car! Have an adult help you with the hot glue.

1 Take two craft sticks. Cut the ends of one to make it a little bit shorter than the other. Cut a straw slightly shorter than one of the sticks and hot glue it to the stick. Repeat with the other craft stick.

2 Trim a bamboo skewer so that it is about 1 to 1½ inches longer on each side than the craft stick (2½–4 centimeters). Hot glue one end of the bamboo stick to the center of a bottle cap. Hold for a few minutes until the glue sets.

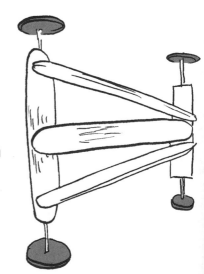

3 Push the other end of the bamboo axle through one of the straws glued to a craft stick. Hot glue a bottle cap to the other end. Put a blob of glue on the bamboo axle on either side of the straw. Make sure the glue doesn't touch the straw. This helps the axle from sliding too far through the straw. Repeat for the second axle.

4 Connect the two wheel bases with a craft stick. Glue two more craft sticks to form the sides of the car. Hold until the glue sets.

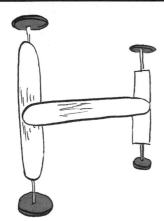

5 Secure a balloon to the end of the third straw with a rubber band. Use masking tape to secure the straw to the car's center craft stick. Make sure the balloon faces forward and the end of the straw faces the rear of the car.

6 Use markers to color and decorate the car.

7 To test your car, blow into the straw and inflate the balloon. Hold your finger over the end of the straw to keep the air in the balloon as you place the car on the floor. Let go and watch the balloon power your car!

TIP: If your car does not move at first, make sure you have fully inflated the balloon. In addition, you may want to give your car a slight nudge to get it started.

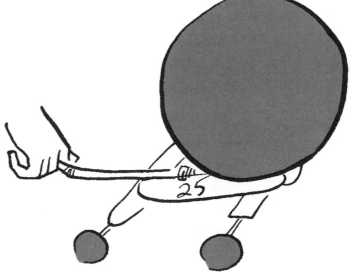

advertise: to make public in a positive way to increase sales.

apprenticeship: the time served as an apprentice.

apprentice: someone who works for a master craftsmen to learn a skill.

aqueduct: a large bridge built to carry water across a valley.

aristocrat: a member of a ruling or wealthy class of people.

artisan: someone who is skilled at a craft.

automated: to operate by machine instead of human labor.

bargain: to work to reach an agreement.

blacklisted: put on a list of people who are considered untrustworthy or not suitable.

boll: the seed pod of the cotton plant that fluffy cotton fibers burst out of.

broadcast: to transmit by radio or television.

canal: a man-made waterway.

capital: money used to start or expand a business.

carbonized: coated with carbon.

carded cotton: cotton that is cleaned and brushed to prepare it for spinning.

chaperone: an adult who protects the safety of young people and makes sure they behave well.

charity: an organization that helps people in need.

combustion: burning fuel to produce energy.

commercially: profitable, to be sold.

competitor: a person or company trying to do the same thing as another.

component: a part.

Congress: a group of people who represent the states and make laws for the country.

consolidate: to join several smaller companies into one larger company.

contract: an agreement, usually including payment of money.

conveyor: a moving belt that carries objects from one place to another in a factory.

corporation: a large company.

cultural icon: a picture, name, face, person, or other image that has meaning for a large group of people.

current: the steady movement of water in a certain direction.

demand: the amount that people want to buy.

disband: to break up or dissolve an organization.

distressed: close to failing.

electrocuted: injured or killed with a severe electric shock.

electromagnetism: magnetism formed by a current of electricity.

enterprising: willing to try a new, risky project.

entrepreneur: a person who starts a business.

exploit: to benefit unfairly from someone else's work.

export: to send something to another country to be sold.

factory: a place where goods are made.

fare: the cost of traveling on a bus, subway, train, plane, boat, or other mode of transportation.

federally sponsored: when the government pays for something.

filament: a very fine wire or thread.

financier: a person who invests large amounts of money in businesses.

financing: the amount of money that an individual or a company has.

flammable: likely to catch fire.

flax: a plant with blue flowers whose fibers are used to make linen.

freight: goods transported by truck, train, ship, or plane.

gin: a tool or mechanical device.

goods: things for sale or to use.

guild: a group of people with a common interest or goal.

GLOSSARY

idle: not working.

incentive: the possibility of a reward that encourages people to do something or work harder.

industrialist: someone who works with businesses and factories.

Industrial Revolution: a time of far-reaching change when the large-scale production of goods began.

industry: the production of goods, especially in factories.

inefficient: wasting time or energy.

ingenuity: inventiveness and originality.

innovation: a new invention or way of doing something.

insulation: material that covers something in order to stop heat or electricity from escaping.

irrigation: supplying water to farmland.

labor union: a group of workers that bargains with the people they work for.

legislation: new laws.

locomotive: an engine used to push or pull railroad cars.

lucrative: profitable and money-making.

manufacture: to make something by machine, in a large factory.

masses: most of the people.

mass produce: to manufacture large amounts of a product.

merchant: someone who buys and sells goods.

militia: a group of citizens who are trained to fight but who only serve in time of emergency.

millwright: a person who builds the machinery of a mill.

mimeograph: a copy machine.

mining: taking minerals from the ground, such as iron ore.

monopoly: when a person or group controls a product or industry.

monotonous: boring and repetitive.

natural resource: materials that occur in nature, such as oil, coal, water, and land.

negotiate: to discuss and reach an agreement.

oil refinery: where oil from the ground is turned into useful products like gasoline.

patent: a right given to only one inventor to manufacture, use, or sell an invention for a certain number of years.

petition: to send a letter signed by many people asking those in power to change something.

philanthropy: helping others by donating money, time, or property.

phonograph: a machine that picks up and reproduces the sounds that have been recorded in the grooves cut into a record.

physics: the study of the universe and how its forces interact with each other.

picket lines: people with signs standing outside to protest. Sometimes they prevented people from entering factories.

plantation: a large farm where crops are grown for sale.

practical: something useful and effective in everyday situations.

production costs: money spent to produce goods.

profit: to make money from business or investments.

prosper: to be successful.

protest: to object to something, often in public.

prototype: the first model of something new.

public works: building of roads, schools, and other projects by a government for the public.

regulation: an official rule or order.

revolutionize: to bring about a far-reaching change.

riot: a gathering of people protesting something, which gets out of control and violent.

royalty: money paid to the inventor of something to use or sell the invention.

rural: in the country.

sabotage: the planned destruction of property, or an act that interferes with work or another activity.

shrewd: able to judge people and situations, and make good decisions.

slum: a run-down place to live.

spindle: the rod on a spinning wheel that twists the thread. The twisted thread is wound around the rod.

strike: when everyone walks off the job.

suburb: an area on or close to the outer edge of a city, usually made up of homes with few businesses.

suit: a complaint against someone in a court of law.

switchboard: the control center or panel for connecting the lines of a telephone system.

tailor: someone who makes, sizes, or repairs clothing.

tenement: a run-down apartment building, especially one that is crowded and in a poor part of a city.

textile: cloth or fabric.

toxic: poisonous.

transcontinental: crossing a continent.

transmit: to send or pass something from one place or person to another.

transport: to move people and goods from one place to another.

trust: property or money that is held or used to benefit others.

turbine: a machine with blades turned by the force of water, air, or steam.

unskilled job: work that does not need much training or education.

urban: in the city.

utility: a basic service supplied to a community, such as telephone, water, gas, or electricity.

vibration: a back and forth movement.

wage: payment for work.

warp: the strong thread that runs vertically in a loom.

work ethic: a set of values that promotes hard work.

working class: people who work in factories and in jobs using their hands.

WEB SITES

www.history.com/topics/industrial-revolution The History Channel. Explore essays, photos, and videos about the Industrial Revolution.

www.nps.gov/lowe/index.htm Lowell National Historical Park.

www.nps.gov/edis/index.htm Thomas Edison National Historical Park. Includes photos and sound recordings.

www.thehenryford.org/museum/index.aspx The Henry Ford Museum. Explore educational topics on the Industrial Revolution, Transportation in America, and American Innovation.

www1.umassd.edu/ir/resources/textileindustry/ Aspects of the Industrial Revolution in Britain. University of Massachussets Dartmouth. Primary source documents about the textile industry.

www.historyteacher.net/APEuroCourse/WebLinks/WebLinks-IndustrialRevolution.htm Links to primary source documents related to the Industrial Revolution.

www.nps.gov/lowe/planyourvisit/upload/mill%20girls.pdf The Mill Girls. Describes daily life for the young women who worked in the Lowell textile mills.

www.womeninworldhistory.com/lesson7.html The Plight of Women's Work in the Early Industrial Revolution in England and Wales.

www.teachersfirst.com/lessons/inventor/ag1.htm Great Inventors of the Industrial Revolution.

www.invent.org/ Invent Now. Learn about inventors and the inventing process.

www.pbs.org/wgbh/theymadeamerica/whomade/innovators_hi.html Who Made America, PBS.org. Biographies of American innovators, including several from the Industrial Revolution.

http://americanhistory.si.edu/ Smithsonian National Museum of American History. View online information about collections and exhibits from the Industrial Revolution.